PRIESTHOOD
IN THE
MODERN WORLD

A READER

A CHURCH BOOK

The **CHURCH** book series from Sheed & Ward focuses on developing discipleship and leadership, fostering faith formation, and moral decision-making, and enhancing the Church's worship and social ministry. Titles in the series address clergy, laity, and religious on topics and issues that concern the whole people of God.

Series Editor: Karen Sue Smith

PRIESTHOOD
IN THE
MODERN WORLD

A READER

Introduction by
Philip J. Murnion

Edited by
Karen Sue Smith

SHEED & WARD
Franklin, Wisconsin

1999

Sheed & Ward
7373 South Lovers Lane Road
Franklin, Wisconsin 53132
1-800-558-0580

Copyright © 1999 by National Pastoral Life Center, 18 Bleecker St., New York, NY 10012

Printed in the United States of America

Cover design: Biner Design

Art direction of interior pages: GrafixStudio, Inc.

Permissions:
"The Priesthood after the Council: Theological Reflections" by M. Edmund Hussey, originally appeared in the Spring 1988 issue of *CHURCH* magazine; "Evolution of the Priesthood: Adapting to Pastoral Needs" by David N. Power, *CHURCH,* Fall 1988, courtesy of *The Furrow,* April 1988; "Making Priesthood Possible: Who Does What and Why?" by Michael J. Himes, *CHURCH,* Fall 1989; "The Practice of Priesthood: Working Through Today's Tensions" by James J. Bacik, *CHURCH,* Fall 1993; "A Ministerial Spirituality: Reflections on Priesthood" by George Niederauer, *CHURCH,* Summer 1991; "Survival Manual for Parish Priests" by Neal E. Quartier, *CHURCH,* Spring 1991; "Taking Responsibility for Hope: One Priest's Prescription" by Thomas J. Morgan, *CHURCH,* Spring 1996; "Priest as Bearer of the Mystery" by Robert E. Barron, *CHURCH,* Summer 1994; "Priest as Doctor of the Soul" by Robert E. Barron, *CHURCH,* Summer 1996; "Ongoing Professional Development: A Ministerial Imperative" by Matthias Neuman, *CHURCH,* Fall 1991; all used with permission of the publisher.

Library of Congress Cataloging-in-Publication Data

Priesthood in the modern world : a reader / introduction by Philip J. Murnion : edited by
    Karen Sue Smith
       p. cm.
    Includes bibliographical references.
    ISBN 1-58051-055-8
    1. Catholic Church—Clergy. 2. Clergy—Office. I. Smith, Karen Sue.
BX1912.P77 1999
262'.142—dc21
                                    98-51555
                                     CIP

1 2 3 4 5 / 02 01 00 99

CONTENTS

INTRODUCTION

Philip J. Murnion

During a recent discussion among priests and bishops in a Midwest province, one priest expressed the fear of a "diminishment" of priesthood, given the increasing reliance on lay people to provide pastoral ministry. His was not a rejection of lay people in ministry but a concern about settling for lay ministry as a substitute for ordained ministry. As the discussion ensued, another priest shared his concern and made it practical by pointing to the prospect that priests would wind up as mostly sacramental ministers, traveling from community to community where lay people provided pastoral care. "How can the ministry of sacraments be regarded as a diminishment of priesthood?" another priest countered. "Isn't sacramental ministry precisely what is most priestly?"

There was not enough time in the meeting to continue the discussion and seek resolution of what seemed to be quite different views among priests who were, nonetheless, in agreement about both the value of lay ministry and the need for the church to address the challenge of providing full Catholic pastoral ministry with fewer priests. To an observer, it seemed as if the two priests actually were more in agreement about priesthood and ministry than the exchange reflected. Surely, the priest who lamented the prospect of a narrowly sacramental ministry would agree that sacramental ministry is unique to priesthood. Yet, he seemed to be saying that what is unique to ordained ministry does not adequately define ordained ministry. Without putting words in his mouth, it may be apt to infer that for him there is something about building up a community of disciples, with all it entails, that is essential to ordained ministry. The sacraments are, to use an old distinction, necessary but are not adequate to make up all the ingredients of that community and, therefore, of pastoral leadership.

I recall that discussion because it exemplifies a wider conversation taking place in the church. The conversation involves answering the question, "What is a priest?" Priesthood is, of course, one element in (a) the church's relationship to the world, (b) the many forms of ministry in the church, and (c) the relationship between hierarchy and community. As the church's relationship to the world undergoes change—the very grounds for Pope John XXIII's convoking of Vatican II—many new forms of ministry proliferate, the number of priests and religious decline, and the church struggles to work out what is distinctive and authoritative about ordained episcopacy and priesthood relative to the priesthood of all the baptized. It is not surprising, then, that ordained priesthood eludes clear and consensual definition.

To be sure, priests go on leading the community in worship; preaching, teaching and ensuring religious formation of the young; providing and arranging pastoral care for those in need and social ministry to further justice; and administering the many ministries and institutions of the church. Yet, when their lives seem much less attractive to young men—and even some of the more assertive women calling for ordination of women speak with disdain of "priesthood as we now know it"—it is not surprising that priests experience failure in reaching agreement about what is essential to ordained priesthood. Indeed, the lack of clarity also makes it difficult to agree about the criteria for admission to seminary and ordination. In other words, priests are remarkably resilient in continuing to develop ministry, even when they feel the burden of defining for themselves the priorities of priestly ministry.

In fact, it may be the problem of establishing priorities of mission rather than defining essentials that is most at stake in the present situation. Though contemporary historians trace the origins of the presbyterate, not directly to any "ordination" at the Last Supper, but to the council of elders around the *episcopos* or bishop, nonetheless it was not long before the three essential elements of ordained priesthood were established: presiding over or administering the sacraments, custody and conveying of the authentic teaching of the church, and linking a local community with the bishop and the universal church. In different periods, one or another of these three essentials was emphasized in response to conditions in the church and/or the influence of what became a religious order. In fact, it was precisely the form given to presbyteral ministry, not the matter that gave definition in the broad sense to priesthood. At times there have been priests who did little or no sacramental ministry while, at other points in history, priests were ordained solely for sacramental ministry. Always the key was what the church needed to ensure its sacramental, formational, and universal dimensions. What is that today?

In the following chapters the authors describe either the evolution of priesthood (David N. Power, M. Edmund Hussey), the changing conditions of pastoral ministry (James J. Bacik, Philip J. Murnion), or a particular aspect of ordained priestly ministry that they regard as needing special attention because it is at the heart of priesthood (Michael J. Himes, Robert E. Barron), because it is urgent for the church, or both. Some authors focus on the priest's own need to be resourceful (Neil E. Quartier, George Niederauer) and responsible for himself (Thomas J. Morgan, Matthias Neuman). The articles focus on the content, character, and context of today's priestly ministry, but do not add up to one neat picture. It is apparent that priesthood will never yield to any definition that restricts priests' ministry to one dimension or service. Nonetheless, I believe that the different views are complementary enough to benefit from and not deny the value of the other's perspective.

In sum, they are all cumulatively hopeful in expressing conviction about the power of priesthood. None even hints that priesthood is passé, an outmoded institution in a post-modern world. The question for all is not "What good is the priesthood?" but "Which goods of priesthood need most to be fostered?" And that perspective is borne out in practice throughout the church today as priests are relentlessly creative in shaping their lives and ministry to fit the needs of the church, and are creatively collaborative as they work through new relationships with lay people and religious on pastoral staffs and councils. Obviously, some priests fail by excessive clericalism or relativism, by misconduct and disrespect, or by otherwise not equipping themselves for the daunting challenge of religious leadership in our age. But these examples of failure are more than offset by the enduring faithfulness, practical pastoral charity, and adaptive creativity of the vast majority of priests. It is as tribute to these priests and as material for mutual reflection among priests that we offer these essays. Those in seminary work and diocesan leadership may also find them invaluable.

—Philip J. Murnion, 1999

COMMON GROUND, HOLY GROUND
A Ministry of Grace and Communion

Philip J. Murnion

The memory is still fresh of Monsignor Ken Velo speaking over the bier of his beloved bishop and friend lying in state within Chicago's Holy Name Cathedral. Ken's words were a veritable psalm, each verse recalling one of the many ways Joseph Bernardin had served his Lord and his church. He concluded each verse with the refrain, "Didn't he teach us? Didn't he show us the way?" No verse of the psalm elicited a deeper response than the one in which he proclaimed: "Didn't he show us that common ground is holy ground?" When he concluded that verse with the refrain, the congregation erupted in applause. And yet a few bishops and cardinals there could not have been comfortable hearing that memorial acclamation. For in this as in no other instance, they had felt the need to find public fault with their brother bishop, questioning the wisdom of his action in such a way as to raise doubts about his fidelity. It had been painful to Cardinal Bernardin, a pain shared by many come to pray over him, and a pain that was now exorcised from among them.

Perhaps his critics were right. Perhaps dialogue would be damaging to the church, encouraging dissent and division that would only undermine the teaching and unity of the church. Whatever the case, the three months from the announcement of the Catholic Common Ground Initiative on August 12, 1996, to the death of Cardinal Bernardin on November 14 were not enough time to work through the dispute and restore the sense of common ground, common faith, and common faithfulness the Cardinal had wished to deepen, not destroy.

The congregation's reaction at the funeral was part of an enormous outpouring of admiration and respect in the last days of the Cardinal's life. It was not just about *common ground;* that term had simply become a symbol for much about his life. The Initiative itself had originated in a pastoral letter by Cardinal Bernardin about parish life in the Archdiocese of Chicago. In that letter he appealed to pastors and parish leaders, in his typically understated way, to foster unity among the many people and varied spiritualities of the parish—the young and the old, lay people and priests, women and men, liturgical spirituality and devotional life.

His pastoral letter was one of many efforts by Cardinal Bernardin to foster mutual respect and unity. Regarding the social teaching of the church, he articulated the "consistent ethic of life" which expressed the church's concern for the sacredness of all life from conception to death, and wove together in common cause those devoted to the elimination of abortion and those involved in other aspects of the church's social mission. He had devoted himself as member, general secretary, and president to building up the National Conference of Catholic Bishops. His talent for fostering consensus was acknowledged by bishops throughout the world, who repeatedly elected him to serve on the council for the triennial synod of bishops in Rome. He worked to strengthen the bonds among Christians and between Christians and Jews.

In the Scriptures we find some texts in which Jesus declares that he has come to divide people from one another, and other texts in which he is clearly trying to foster unity. In the church, and between the church and the culture, Joseph Bernardin was a prime exemplar of those who look for points of unity without sacrificing the integrity of the gospel, the church, or themselves.

Another way he exemplified this approach was his ability to recognize and draw on the gifts and talents of others in the church. He called on some for spiritual guidance, others for theological expertise, some for their writing ability, others for their organizational genius. A story is told that early in the pontificate of John Paul II, Karl Rahner was informed by a fellow Jesuit that the pope was busy writing his first encyclical. Rahner is reported to have commented that it was not proper for a pope to write his own encyclicals, for his teaching is not simply his private wisdom, but the best of the wisdom of the church. In more recent years, stories have it that the pope has drawn on the talents and wisdom of many people in preparing his encyclicals. Joseph Bernardin regularly did the same, drawing on the wisdom and talents of many people. This is not simply good management style or a personality characteristic. It reflects an ecclesiology, an appreciation of the many gifts and charisms in the church. It is the task of bishops and others in church leadership to recognize the many gifts in the church, bring them forth, and draw them together for the good of the church. The pastoral letter on peace which Cardinal Bernardin shepherded through the conference of bishops provided an outstanding example of this, setting a model of consultation that recognized both the varieties of expertise in church and society, and the wisdom found in the ordinary people of the church, while carefully protecting both the teaching of the church and the teaching role and authority of the bishop.

A bishop who worked with Joseph Bernardin many years earlier once remarked that he had never seen a more political man: Bernardin approached every decision in light of how it would affect a whole range of people. Though the biography of Cardinal Spellman, published with his approval while he was alive, portrayed him as a very political man, calling a bishop political is usually regarded as an insult. But being political has many meanings. The term can be used to describe someone seeking his own advancement, currying favor with superiors to gain higher positions in the church. In spite of Paul's view that it is a worthy thing to aspire to be a bishop, being political in these terms can indeed be quite unworthy; it can place self-promotion ahead of service to the gospel, or mistake one for the other. If one prefers status to mission, it becomes clear when personal aspirations are thwarted. The result can be a withering of the soul. If the mission is paramount, however, it can be pursued from any position.

In other respects it is quite admirable to be political. This is the case when being political means practicing the art of the possible, building consensus, trying to be practical and sensitive to all the constituencies and personalities affected by one's actions or statements. It means being as inclusive as possible of the many concerns and viewpoints at stake in a situation. Being political in this sense is to stand somewhere between prophecy and bureaucracy. On the one hand it means placing oneself between those who, by taking a sharply defined position on an issue of principle, challenge and divide people and, on the other hand, those who mistake rigid adherence to existing laws and regulations as tantamount to preserving the values those rules were meant to protect. Being political entails trying to achieve the best of principle through adaptation of the resources of the institution. Political in this case can be another name for pastoral.

In what respect was Joseph Bernardin political? I did not know him well enough in his earlier years to say. Maybe he was moved by mission, maybe his motives were mixed, maybe his was a politics of ambition. Whatever the truth, he acknowledged how much he had to grow as a disciple of the Lord and as a bishop. It seems fair to assert that he became the quintessential expression of political as pastoral. In doing so, his deliberate steps to achieve consensus could disappoint those impatient with the status quo and threaten those unduly bound to the status quo. Eventually his pastoral approach became prophetic, for there are three elements to prophecy: revelation, proclamation, and incarnation. As an agent of God's revelation, the prophet helps us more clearly to see our lives as the Lord sees them. The prophet's proclamation then confronts the world with this truth in a way that challenges people's assumptions. Finally, the prophet incarnates the message as his own life becomes a symbol of his message. Joseph Bernardin shed new light on the opportunities and obligations of reconciliation in church and society. In doing so he challenged those who would deepen church divisions either by dissipating truth and Tradition through relativism, or by reducing the range of acceptable truth through integralism. Eventually, he became the message of reconciliation in his own life by the way he handled false allegations and was reunited in the Eucharist with his accuser, and by the way he became reconciled to death, his "friend."

It was a hard journey; Bernardin passed through many fires purifying his motives, his priorities, and his lifestyle. No sooner had the trials occasioned by the false accusation passed than he was invaded by cancer. A bishop who suffered cancer years earlier confessed that it had taken him a year to accept the fact that God would allow such suffering when he had been so single-minded in devotion to the mission of Christ and the church. Surely Cardinal Bernardin had at least a flicker of such Garden of Olives doubt. Joseph Bernardin's life ended amid as much public rejection as acclamation. Ultimately, however, his life and death and final testimony conveyed the conviction expressed in the final words of Bernanos's country priest: "Does it matter? Grace is everywhere...."

It is not surprising, then, that after telling me on August 29, 1996 (just two weeks after announcing the Catholic Common Ground Initiative) that the cancer had returned and his days were numbered, he pledged to do as much as he could in the time remaining to further the cause of the Initiative. It had become a metaphor for his life's work of building the unity of the church so that it could better serve the mission of Christ. What was metaphor would become legacy.

It is possible for us priests to draw some lessons from this legacy—lessons about our personal dispositions, our theological assumptions, and our sense of mission—and apply them to our continuing personal, presbyteral, and pastoral development.

QUALITIES OF A COMMON GROUND EFFORT AS EXEMPLIFIED IN THE LIFE AND WORK OF CARDINAL BERNARDIN

Listening

Central to the message of the Catholic Common Ground Initiative is the call to dialogue: speaking to one another. It has become clear to me and others working to build on the Cardinal's legacy expressed in Catholic Common Ground that perhaps more important than dia-*logue* is di-*audition*— i.e., *listening* to one another and enabling one another to listen. This requires that we clear the ground of obstacles to hearing one another, to hearing the message of the Gospel, to being open to the truth. This begins in ourselves. One of the most poignant responses to the call of the Initiative came from a professor of moral theology who wrote that he took it as a challenge to himself: Was he honestly presenting to his students the views of those he disagreed with? He urged his students to call him on this.

We priests need to put aside our prejudices and stereotypes so that we can truly hear what others are saying. In the foundational statement of the Initiative, *Called to Be Catholic*, the ground rules for dialogue are mostly about how we must listen to one another. They caution against dismissive labels like "radical feminism" or "the hierarchy";

against looking immediately for the holes in another's argument; against instinctively imputing unworthy motives or disloyalty to another; against adopting the view that we are in complete and sole possession of all truth. In a splendid example of implementing the call to common ground, a four-part workshop was conducted at the annual convention of The National Association of Pastoral Musicians. Sheila McLoughlin, who led the workshop, reported that it was not until the third session that the seventy participants really listened to one another and began to hear the differing views of worship and the values at stake. They had to overcome the temptation to trump one another and to see every opinion voiced as an occasion for retort. When true listening took hold, the session became a spiritual experience for the participants, an experience of grace and communion.

There are programs and processes throughout our society, in business and industry, designed to increase people's ability to listen. For ourselves, there is probably no better preparation for listening than prayer—our effort to hear God, to hear our own minds and hearts in the enhanced mode that prayer offers. Participants in the first Cardinal Bernardin Conference sponsored by the Initiative in March 1997 pointed to time united in Eucharist and prayer as essential conditions that enable us in the course of the weekend to listen to one another and then to speak to one another in a new way.

After attention to ourselves, we need to provide opportunities and structures for others to feel they will be listened to. We need to create the space that allows people to trust. When they express themselves, they must know they are on solid ground. They are not in jeopardy; their identity and integrity are not threatened if their views are challenged, their feelings are exposed, or they find themselves at odds with others. People need to feel they are respected, their good faith is presumed, and their desire to be faithful to the Lord is as great as our own. It also means considering how people will hear us when we make statements—what they may find offensive, insensitive, or simply confusing in our language.

This disposition in our approach to others involves a whole theology and understanding of mission. First, a word about the theology.

A Pastoral Theology

The pursuit of common ground is rooted in a theology of church and revelation. It is based on the belief that the wisdom of the Spirit of God is communicated to the whole people of God. In *Lumen Gentium* we find the teaching: "The Spirit dwells in the Church and in the hearts of the faithful, as in a temple, prays and bears witness in them that they are his adoptive children. He guides the church in the way of all truth and, uniting it in fellowship and ministry, bestows upon it different hierarchic and charismatic gifts, and in this way directs it and adorns it with his fruits" (LG I.4).

Listening to others and making it a point to draw on the wisdom of others is not, as some construe it, a concession to the populist demands of our culture. It is not a tactic to win acceptance for a teaching or policy or practice. Rather, it is a requirement for the development of teaching and policy and practice. Without listening we do not penetrate as much of the truth as the church has been given.

We need to be hearers of the word before we can be preachers of the word. Our need to listen to one another and to develop forums and councils, prayerful communities and groups, is an essential part of our understanding of church. The synod of the Americas held in Rome, November 16–December 12, 1997, and the consultations that preceded it, are an example of this ecclesiology. Given the needs of the time and the urgency of being faithful to the ecclesiology of Vatican II, the working paper for the synod reported two aspects of this need; namely, the tactical and the theological.

First, the tactical: "In order to overcome divisions, the replies to the *lineamenta* speak of the necessity of fostering ecclesial structures and personal attitudes which facilitate dialogue. Many suggest initiating joint programs in pastoral activities on the national, diocesan, and parochial levels."

The paragraph goes on but shifts, intentionally or not, to the theological: "To do this, the responses indicate a necessity to encourage an open-mindedness in accepting the collaborating of all members of the people of God, especially the laity, who can enrich the dialogue and pastoral reflection with their charisms and ministries" (par 39). In other words, beyond the need to overcome division is the need to draw on the charisms and ministries of the faithful if the dialogue is to be enriched.

Guided by the Teaching

There is another aspect to the theology of listening. The theology that recognizes the gifts of the Spirit distributed throughout the church, and indeed beyond, also recognizes the primal place of the magisterium in teaching and the obligation we have to listen carefully to the teaching of the church. In the words of *Lumen Gentium*:

There is only one Spirit who, according to his own richness and the needs of the ministries, gives his various gifts for the welfare of the church. Among these gifts the primacy belongs to the grace of the apostles to whose authority the Spirit himself subjects even those who are endowed with charisms (*LG* I.7).

In the words of the Initiative statement:

[O]ur discussion must be accountable to the Catholic tradition and the Spirit-filled, living church that brings to us the revelation of God in Jesus. . . . Authentic accountability rules out a fundamentalism that narrows the richness of the tradition to a text or decree, and it rules out a narrow appeal to individual or contemporary experience that ignores the cloud of witnesses over the centuries or the living magisterium of the church exercised by the bishops and the Chair of Peter.

One example of polarization the Catholic Common Ground Initiative was meant to offset was the tendency to choose between hierarchy and collegiality, the right wing choosing hierarchy, the left collegiality. The theology undergirding Common Ground is in this respect and so many others a both/and, not an either/or ecclesiology. To those who see the revelation that grounds the church and the wisdom that guides the church conveyed only through the hierarchy, the invitation to dialogue seems a threat to authentic unity. To those committed to unrelieved egalitarianism, the Initiative's insistence on accountability to the magisterium and adherence to the boundaries of authentic teaching seems an unwarranted restriction.

There is a burden on the magisterium as on the entire church to consider the challenge of listening when speaking. This means not only listening to the Spirit as it speaks through the church but also considering how people will hear what is being taught. Doesn't St. Paul's

admonishment about being sensitive to what scandalizes and drives
people away from church apply here? He was talking about what nourishes the body; we are talking about what nourishes the spirit. The language of church statements and the stance of the teachers must enable
people to hear what is being taught, not only avoiding terms that are
unnecessarily distracting or offensive, but also evincing respect for the
best intentions of the members of the church and using a language that
speaks to the minds and hearts of the people.

Synods and councils and other forums are not just mechanisms
ancillary to the work of the church; they are themselves expressions of
what it means to be church. The effort to bring together people of
varying viewpoints and concerns is an essential part of expressing and
building up the body of Christ. In effect, the pursuit of common
ground is based on the assumption of communion, on the belief that
we are bound together in the Lord through the Spirit of Christ in ways
that are not of our doing. We are called to achieve and express in the
communities of the church what has been accomplished for us in
Christ and realized in us through our baptism into the Body of Christ.
It is to make the communities we fashion expressions of the communion the Lord has formed. We are then servants of God's grace.

The Mission

Ultimately, what is a personal stance is not only a theology but also a
mission. It is perhaps the lack of a shared mission that most accounts
for the divisions in the church and what lies behind the reluctance of
young men to give themselves to the priesthood.

Central to the mission of the church in our time is the effort to
build up the community of disciples. It is not just to engage individuals
in the sacramental life of the church; it is not just to form individuals
in the faith; it is not just to care for individuals and alleviate individual
distress or even to find ways to promote justice. It is to build a community of worship, a community of faith, a community of charity and justice. It is to bring people together in the experience of God's love and
in the paschal mystery of Jesus' triumph over death. It is to promote
reconciliation of people not only between themselves and their Lord
but also with the community of conscience that is the church. It is to
engage people in the kinds of mutual care, peer ministry, and coalitions

for justice which embody in themselves the kind of culture and society they seek to promote.

A recent study of communities of women religious concludes that the communities most successful at attracting and keeping members are those, liberal or conservative, who carry out their commitment to community in their ministries and their living arrangements. They are engaged in a shared work, not just shared values, and in common life, not just commitment to one another. We can find what is true of religious orders in the pastoral life of the church as well. Where do we find the greatest vitality in parish life? It is where the approach goes beyond providing sacraments, formation, and care to individuals by fostering community in worship, community in formation, and community in the works of charity and justice.

Let's be more specific. One of the most dramatic reversals of a trend has occurred in adult initiation into the church. In 1960, 145,000 adults became Catholic. That figure plunged to 75,000 in 1974, the end of what we call the sixties. By 1994 the number of adults received into the church had soared to 162,000. What made the difference? Not just the end of the sixties, but the implementation of the rite of adult initiation. This is a rite situated within the community of worship whose process involves a community of fellow seekers, sponsors, and catechists who accompany the candidates on the journey. It culminates not only in the Easter Vigil ceremony of full incorporation but in the mystagogic introduction to service of the community. It begins in community, its process is communal, its goal is the community.

Regarding evangelization, which I define as formation in faith that makes a difference in people's lives, there has been no more significant development than the formation of small communities in parishes—communities of faith and prayer, of mutual reflection on the Scriptures and shared learning of the teaching of the church, of observe-judge-act process that enables people to address causes and not simply consequences of problems. Recent reports show hundreds of thousands of Catholics in these communities, mostly within parishes. No parish renewal program has been more helpful to the life of the church in recent decades than Renew, which emphasizes small communities. Nor has there been any better effort to reach out to Catholics estranged from the church community—which is what some mean when they talk about evangelization—than the small communities of Renew and other forms of small communities that invite people into a comfortable and accepting community of faith.

Finally, the mission of justice is exercised in the formation of community organizations: coalitions of parishes, Catholic and other, through which people come together to tackle challenges of their community such as adequate housing and neighborhood safety, quality education for their children and crime prevention, economic development and good health services. The community acts, not just the leaders of local institutions. The goal is the formation of a just, mutually respectful, and caring community, not just the solving of problems. And the church, through programs such as The Campaign for Human Development, stands as a powerful force in the formation of these community organizations.

Such vitality can be seen in many other ways as well. It exists in parishes that provide the Eucharist but also engage the assembly in common prayer and the experience of reconciliation. It is found in parishes that provide pastoral care from the staff but also encourage support groups of the bereaved, the separated and divorced, the unemployed, the addicted, and others with similar interests or needs— opportunities for people to minister to one another. It is seen in parishes that engage their members in councils and assemblies to plan their mission as a community of faith. It is in parishes that make room for a variety of spiritualities and concerns. This community style of parish is the place where the mission of Christ and his church becomes an expression and experience of hope.

What we have seen as a personal style rooted in conciliar theology is in fact the mission. The mission is the building of community as shared intimacy in the love and mercy of God, shared fellowship in caring for one another, and social solidarity as agents of transformation so that the Kingdom of God may be more evident in our cities and towns. In such a church people feel their lives have been heard by the preacher and can therefore hear both the consolation and the demands of the Gospel, where fragmentation by race and income and ideology can be overcome, and where the community of discipleship supports the courage of discipleship. All is communion.

Personal, Priestly, and Pastoral Challenges

What does this say to priests? Many things. Consider some personal,
presbyteral, and pastoral consequences of this understanding of the
church's mission.

First, personal challenges. There is no more powerful personal
quality of priests than hospitality. Hospitality makes people feel welcome, whatever their situation. In an address to a group of bishops,
Pope John Paul II described a parish as "a home where the members of
the Body of Christ . . . accept their brothers and sisters . . . whatever
their condition or origins." Fostering this begins with the priest. The
now-dated but still useful Notre Dame Study of Catholic Parish Life
found that, in part, people will experience their parish as a community
if the pastor knows their names. Similarly, the confessor who is kind
can give new vitality to the sacrament of reconciliation.

We are more likely to enable people to experience the love and
forgiveness of God if we have experienced it ourselves. You may know
Alice Miller's book with the somewhat misleading title, *The Drama of
the Gifted Child* (Basic Books, 1981). A more descriptive title might be
"The Primal Need for Acceptance." The point of the book is that if a
child does not experience unconditional love in the very earliest days
and years, but rather is forced to serve the emotional needs of mother
and father, that child will always suffer some feeling of inadequacy, will
always be unsure and defensive, will never be able to be generous in
loving others. We are that child. If we do not find ways to experience
love and forgiveness, we will have great difficulty extending them to
others. We will be impatient listening to others. Our needs will be too
great to be open to the needs of others, our need for self-esteem too
great to recognize the gifts and talents of others.

We must be listeners, listeners to the Word, listeners to the lives
of people, listeners to what the culture is saying. To hear the Word and
to hear the lives of people requires not only one-to-one experiences. It
requires reading—reading that helps us understand the Scriptures and
the teaching of the church, reading (e.g., good novels or biographies)
that helps us understand what people are going through, and reading
that helps us understand the culture. Such reading is like tuning ourselves to be better instruments of ministry. In Stephen Covey's language, it is "sharpening the saw." Good theology, good spirituality,

good canon law make room for a rich variety of expressions without sacrificing what is normative.

In his letter to priests, *Pastores Dabo Vobis,* John Paul II notes that priesthood is fundamentally relational and urges priests to continue to develop basic human and relational qualities, to deepen spirituality and intellectual capacities, and to learn and hone pastoral skills. In short, the priest is encouraged to develop ways in which he can listen to the heartbeat of his parish and times and find ways he can enter into and develop community with the people whom he serves. Priests must be continually learning, listening, and developing people.

Presbyteral Development

Next, consider a few presbyteral consequences. Priesthood has been traced back to the role of the presbyter. Some want to restore this title for priests. In the earliest days of the church, the title of priest posed a problem where it was important to distinguish church leaders from the Hebrew priesthood and to underscore the one priesthood of Jesus. Since this is not our situation today, I don't find the title *priest* a problem, and the title *presbyter* is neither attractive in our language nor likely to take hold. But it is precisely the presbyteral dimension of ordained priesthood, namely, serving as counselor to the bishop, that I wish to underscore here. To be a priest connects us in a special way to the sacraments of course, but it also links us in a special way to the bishop.

A newspaper account reported that a group of pastors in Chicago delivered a memorandum to their new archbishop, indicating both their respect and their concern about some of his early statements and actions, which they felt might not be helpful. The memo was released to the press by a conservative group seeking to corner the archbishop and force him to take a rigid stand regarding pastoral practices. It was unfortunate the memo was leaked to the press and, in light of the intentions of those who did so, it was unsuccessful. For the pastors to have composed and sent the memo to the archbishop was, I think, to act responsibly as presbyters. Too often priests can adopt a passive-aggressive stance, murmuring discontent and never addressing the causes directly with one another or with the bishop. It may be that a bishop has made it clear that he does not want to hear what the priests are thinking on a range of issues. Of course, the presbyteral councils are meant to be the essential means for priests to play their original presbyteral role. These will need to be further developed, and the bishop must provide not only the personal encouragement but also the structure by which this can happen. But in every way, there must be means for listening to one another.

We need also to review what we discuss and how well we discuss these subjects in our councils. Before he died, Cardinal Bernardin wrote to a number of national organizations such as the National Federation of Priests Councils, asking them to consider whether the Initiative statement, *Called to Be Catholic*, was relevant to their work. Some indicators suggest that presbyteral councils, as key forums for dialogue in the church, may be more successful addressing management issues, such as plans for staffing parishes, than ministry issues, such as the quality of worship or the roles of women or concrete ways for the church to bring the gospel into public life. It may be that priests councils do not address issues such as the qualities essential to parish life. But each one will have to be a judge of that.

An occasion when I reflected with a presbyteral council on how they function suggests several points for consideration. Together we reviewed subjects the council had discussed well, subjects they had discussed poorly (i.e., with no satisfactory conclusion), and subjects they did not discuss at all. Their best discussions concerned management issues, for example, plans for staffing parishes, priests' stipends, diocesan fund-raising, and so on. The issues they discussed poorly were those too vague, never posed, or focused in such a way as to make it impossible to reach clear conclusions, for example, the morale of priests. The councils rarely if ever discussed broader or deeper pastoral issues, for example, the qualities needed for good worship, the goals and programs for religious education, or women in the church. The factors that militated against such discussions seemed to be meetings that were too infrequent, too brief, or dominated by management issues; the absence of adequate preparation; a fear of getting into discussions where sharp theological differences might emerge with little hope of reconciliation; and inadequate staffing of the council. If presbyteral councils are to provide or promote diocesan dialogue about urgent issues in church life, these factors have to be addressed.

Those involved in the Initiative have concluded that a few elements are essential for good dialogue on many critical issues. These include a context of prayer, focus on a critical issue clearly stated, inclusion of a variety of viewpoints on the issue, a procedure that provides for careful listening to one another, and a clear intent to learn from and further the pastoral mission of the church.

One other concern regarding the relationship between priests and their bishops bears comment. The ways a bishop and his priests relate to movements and special groups in a diocese can affect the solidarity of priests and bishop. Movements and special groups, new religious orders, and new expressions of renewal are ways followers of Christ focus on a particular aspect of the church they wish to promote or protect. They have been and continue to be important sources of vitality to the church. These movements and orders, however, must always be seen as ancillary to the basic ministry of the local church. They cause difficulty when it appears they enjoy greater trust and honor and are more readily listened to than those who labor in the parishes and other diocesan ministries.

Pastoral

Our style of parish is territorial, sacramental, and comprehensive. In a sense these words are redundant. For to describe a parish as territorial is to say that everything that happens in a community is part of the life and obligation of a parish. It is to express in structure what is constitutional to church, as stated in the opening words of *Gaudium et Spes:* "The joys and hopes, the grief and anguish of the people of our time, especially of those who are poor or afflicted, are the joys and hopes, the grief and anguish of the followers of Christ as well. Nothing that is genuinely human fails to find an echo in their hearts" (GS, 1). A more felicitous expression of this same sentiment may be found in an address by John Paul II to a group of French bishops: "If we are imbued with the grace of faith, enlivened by hope, and inspired by charity, there is no happy or sad aspect of village or neighborhood which can fail to move us. Thus evangelization will take different forms in social solidarity, family life, work, neighborly relations." To use the term territorial is to say that all of life is sacred.

To describe a parish as sacramental is to say that God works through the material realities of life, that everything from birth to death is caught up in the life-generating love of God.

To call a parish comprehensive is to say that everything that involves living concerns the parish, even the lives of those, Catholic or other, who do not gather for the Eucharist. This is our boast and our burden, and perhaps what most distinguishes the Catholic parish in the United States. This extensive style of parish requires broadly collaborative leadership. It also requires commitment to stewardship both because the responsibility of any staff is to engage the parishioners themselves in the concerns of community and mission of the parish, and because the community cannot provide fair wages and just conditions to the needed staff without broad support and commitment from the whole parish. Parishioners will acknowledge and assume more responsibility for the community and mission of the church when they are listened to and respected. Furthermore, they support their parishes financially when they are involved. Consequently, engaging people in practical ways not only encourages their responsibility for one another but also makes financial support of the parish's required staff more likely.

In short, pastoral structures should strive to be inclusive, communal, and collaborative. Generous and open to all, they will offer hospitality to everyone in the reliable way parishes can, despite changes in pastors and staffs, neighborhoods, or people's interests.

CONCLUSION

Cardinal Bernardin called Catholics to work toward common ground, which means reaffirming and promoting "the full range of *authentic unity, acceptable diversity,* and *respectful dialogue,* not just as a way to dampen conflict but as a way to make our conflicts constructive, and ultimately as a way to understand the meaning of discipleship of Jesus Christ."

Priests are the ones who, more than anyone else in the church, make space for this common ground. For priests are a sign that believers are united not in a philosophy but in a person, not in private devotion but in the public Eucharist. Priests bring together the teaching of the church and the faith of the people. Priests link the words of the lectionary with the language of the people. Priests provide the opportunity for reconciliation in the context of God's mercy. Priests assemble many races and nationalities, cultures and generations, in one community.

Movements come and go, specializations emerge and disappear, priorities change with the times, but when the history of this era is written, I believe the fidelity of priests in pastoral ministry will be counted as the assurance of continuity in what was an age of discontinuity. It will be seen that the priest in pastoral ministry maintained the tradition and adapted to the present, provided for daily demands and laid the ground for the opportunities of the future.

When the Catholic Common Ground Initiative was announced, Andrew Greeley supported the initiative but criticized the analysis. He argued that polarization is a problem of the elites not the parishes. Insofar as he is accurate, it is because priests have done what the homilist described at Cardinal Bernardin's funeral: They have made it clear that common ground is holy ground, where the Spirit of God brings together all the gifts of the church, all the wonders of a grace-filled communion.

THE PRIESTHOOD AFTER THE COUNCIL
Theological Reflections

M. Edmund Hussey

Sister Ann Simeon was my seventh-grade teacher. She died this past summer and our diocesan newspaper reported she was ninety-five years old, which surprised me quite a bit since I had assumed she was ninety-five years old when I was in the seventh grade.

In fact, she was an excellent teacher, one of the very best, and a lovely person. She had an enormous influence on most of her students, myself included.

Sister Ann Simeon was a great promoter of vocations to the priesthood, as were most of the nuns of that era. She knew exactly what the priesthood meant and she was very clear about the identity of the priest. The priest was truly another Christ, an *alter Christus,* who spoke in the name of Christ. As Christ on earth, the priest said to infants: "I baptize you," and to sinners: "I absolve you." Above all, at Mass the priest stood in the person of Christ and said over the bread and the wine: "This is *my* body; this is the cup of *my* blood." I remember Sister Ann Simeon telling us that the priest could call God down from heaven to the altar, that only the priest could do this, that no one else in the world had the power to do this.

Many of us were naturally quite impressed and thought seriously about the possibility of becoming priests. But Sister Ann Simeon was a realist, not a starry-eyed visionary, and she told us plainly that there were also costs, great costs, if we were to enter the seminary. We had to be good students, willing to study for many years. We would have to live a very disciplined life. We should not expect to become wealthy. We would not even have a home of our own and would have to go to whatever parish the bishop sent us. Above all, we would have to give up marriage and a family of our own.

Sister Ann Simeon's vivid and dramatic presentation of the priesthood was, in fact, a very sound, reasonable, and orthodox one. It was solidly based on the Tridentine theology that emphasized the priesthood as the principal ministry in the church, and whose starting point was the sacramental powers that belong to the priest alone and that set him apart from the laity. The principal sacramental power was, of course, the power to change the bread and wine into the body and blood of Christ. To quote a medieval Latin formula, the priest had the *potestas en Corpus Christi eucharisticum.*

ALTER EPISCOPUS

The Tridentine era of the church ended in October 1958, less than five months after my own ordination to the priesthood. On October 9 of that year, Eugenio Pacelli, known to the world as Pope Pius XII, died at Castel Gandolfo. On October 28, Angelo Guiseppe Roncalli was elected Pope John XXIII in the Sistine Chapel. John XXIII called a council that would take a new look and, as it turned out, a non-Tridentine look at the church and the world.

This new council, the Second Vatican Council, did not emphasize the priesthood as the principal ordained ministry in the church. Instead the council documents clearly state that the priest participates in the ministry of the bishop, that the priest takes the place of the bishop in the parish, and that the priest depends on the bishop in the exercise of his ministry. The *alter Christus* has become the *alter Episcopus.* I suspect that not even many bishops would argue that this change should be considered a promotion. The priest as an *alter Episcopus* inevitably makes dramatically new demands on the relationship between the bishop and the priest. In the Tridentine church, when the priest was an *alter Christus,* the relationship between the priest and the bishop was not a crucial factor in the priest's happiness in his vocation. Even an unreasonable and erratic bishop could generally be avoided; he might even serve as a source of much amusement at clerical gatherings. After all, an *alter Christus*, one who is another Christ, could rather easily survive estrangement from a mere bishop. But an *alter Episcopus* cannot.

Important as the Second Vatican Council's emphasis on the bishop was, its emphasis on the whole church, on the people as the church, was even more important. Instead of beginning its discussion of the church with the hierarchy, *Lumen Gentium* begins by emphasizing that the church is fundamentally and basically the entire community of believers. Although this emphasis seems almost trite when stated so baldly, its implications are enormous. I shall mention only two of those that have been of great importance for priests.

First, if the church was the entire community of believers, then the liturgy of the church could no longer be a spectator sport at which the people watched someone else do something for them. The liturgy had to become once again the public work of all the people. No longer could I be a priest so that others did not have to be priests; I had to be a priest in order to enable the entire community to be a priestly people, a worshipping church, a eucharistic community. No longer could I say Mass that others heard, or even celebrate Mass at which others assisted. Instead, the entire community must now celebrate a liturgy at which I would preside.

Second, if the church was the entire community, then the work of the church was not my responsibility as a priest, but was the responsibility of the people of God, of all the baptized. No longer could I feel that I was entrusted with the mission of the church in a special way and that the people should support me in my work. I now had to realize that the mission of the church is the responsibility of all who are baptized, and that I have been ordained to support them in their work.

Therefore, Vatican II called priests, not as a priestly caste endowed with special powers, but primarily as baptized Christians, and only then as those who have been ordained to serve the community of believers.

The Council of Trent summarized its teaching on the priesthood by characterizing it as the power of consecrating the true Body and Blood of Christ and of remitting or retaining sins. But Vatican II, in "The Ministry and Life of Priests" (*Presbyterorum Ordinis*) does not even mention the priestly power of consecrating the bread and wine. Instead, it begins with a discussion of the priesthood of the faithful and then speaks about all ministry in the church as a means of enabling the church to be the one body of Christ.

Presbyterorum Ordinis affirms that the basic ministry in the church belongs to the bishop, whose "ministerial role has been handed down to priests in a limited degree." This document teaches that the bishop fully possesses the priesthood of Christ (in the sacramental order), while the priest participates in that priesthood in a derived and dependent manner. The bishop is the sign of Christ to his flock, while the priest is a sign of the bishop.

Now it is important to remember that *Presbyterorum Ordinis* is not one of the more significant documents of Vatican II. In fact, the bishops of the council somewhat took the priesthood for granted and did not feel that there was much need to discuss the matter at great length. But indirectly and unwittingly, they severely undermined the traditional role and significance of the priest in the church. By insisting that the bishop is the primary minister in the church and that the priest is the helper of the bishop, the council demoted the priest from an *alter Christus* to an *alter Episcopus*. And by emphasizing the priesthood of the laity and de-emphasizing the sacred power that set the priest apart from the laity, the council deprived the priest of his traditional identity and clear self-image.

In hindsight, and it is only in hindsight, the recent decline in the number of priests and their present straits is the natural and perhaps even inevitable result of the documents of the Second Vatican Council.

In Transition

The Second Vatican Council's emphases on the church as the entire community, on the priesthood of all the baptized, and on the pastoral ministry of the bishop in the church are all theologically sound and are valuable corrections to some off-balance views that had prevailed for centuries. The fact that these new emphases have caused great turmoil in priestly ministry should in no way suggest that they are, therefore, unhealthy or unsound developments. In fact, I am convinced that they are positive and enormously valuable steps forward. But the fact also remains that they have raised important questions not only for priests but for the entire church, questions that I believe have not as yet been able to be addressed sufficiently and satisfactorily.

There is no question that the priestly office and the priest's own understanding of his office are in a period of great transition. The

Tridentine image still survives, of course, but it is no longer taken for granted and indeed is even challenged by many. Yet no new image has acquired clear enough outlines to take its place. Karl Rahner has insisted that the priestly office in the church has been and continues to be an extremely complex reality. He cautions against any attempts to reduce this full reality to only one of its basic elements or characteristics.

And so, rather than make a futile attempt to present a neatly packaged theology of the priesthood, I would merely like to suggest two theological principles and five concrete characteristics of our priesthood as we actually live it. I will not, of course, develop them fully but only present them briefly.

TWO PRINCIPLES

My first theological principle concerns the relationship between the ordained priesthood and the priesthood of the faithful. In order to avoid a simplistic identification of the priesthood of the baptized and the priesthood of the ordained, church documents, ordination homilies, and theological articles frequently appeal to *Lumen Gentium* to affirm that they differ from one another not only in degree but also in essence. But I want to point out to you that the sentence from *Lumen Gentium* that is cited to support this essential difference actually affirms a close connection between the two and merely presumes the essential difference.

In the Abbott edition of the council documents the sentence reads: "Although they differ from one another in essence and not only in degree, the common priesthood of the faithful and the hierarchical priesthood are nonetheless interrelated."

Consequently, although we must not deny the essential difference between the two, it may be that the difference ought not to be overemphasized and used as the starting point for developing a theology of the priesthood. In fact, I believe that a search for the essential difference between the two as a starting point for understanding the ordained priesthood may complicate the issue unnecessarily. I would suggest that the principal affirmation of that sentence in *Lumen Gentium*, the interrelatedness of the priesthood of the faithful and the hierarchical priesthood, might be a better starting point. It might then be easier to see that the ordained priesthood does not intrude between

God and the priesthood common to all the faithful, but instead enables the priesthood of the faithful to be fulfilled and effective.

My second theological principle concerns the relationship between the priest and the bishop, and it is somewhat similar to my first principle. Just as an overemphasis on the essential difference between the priesthood of the faithful and the priesthood of the ordained creates unnecessary difficulties, so also I believe that an over-stated attempt to separate the bishop and the priest will create other unnecessary difficulties.

In fact, throughout much of our history the exact relationship between the episcopacy and the priesthood has been a matter of some dispute. In the immediate past, in the Tridentine era, the bishop was seen essentially as a priest, but with two additional sacramental powers, the power to ordain and the power to confirm. The post-Vatican II church no longer tends to see the bishop in terms of the priest, but tends to see the priest in terms of the bishop. In the Tridentine church the bishop was a "priest plus." In the post-Vatican II church, the priest is a "bishop minus."

FIVE CHARACTERISTICS

While leaving aside right now a complete development of this point, I do want to state the fairly generally accepted theological principle that the priesthood is not radically separate from the episcopacy. My next points confirm that principle, for I now wish to list five concrete characteristics of our priesthood as we actually live it. These characteristics, which also have application to the episcopacy, are absolutely essential for an understanding of the priesthood.

First of all, by virtue of our ordination, we priests have a presidential role in the church. We preside at the assemblies of the church, and we are presidents of local churches in a very real sense, especially if we are pastors of parishes. The bishop, too, is the president of a local church, a local church that we call a diocese rather than a parish.

It is important to remember that in the early church there was no distinction between a parish and a diocese. Most cities of the ancient world were small towns by our standards. Thessalonica, Ephesus, and Corinth were more akin to our small Midwestern county seats than to our major cities. The Christians in these cities belonged to one ecclesial community, to one local church presided over by an *epis-copus*, assisted by a council of *presbyteroi*, and served by one or more *diakonoi*. The gradual development of parishes and the consequent distinction between parishes and dioceses may be one of the most important and least studied developments in our ecclesial structures.

At any rate, the local church of the New Testament and the subapostolic era has no exact correspondence in today's church. Legally or canonically the local church today is the diocese, and only the bishop is empowered to ordain and thus provide for the continuing life of the church. However, the parish is the real local church for most Catholics, for the parish is where they gather to celebrate the Eucharist, where they are baptized and married, and where their funeral liturgies are celebrated. It is in the parish that they learn the tradition of Christianity, and it is from the parish that they derive spiritual nourishment for their lives and their work.

Second, by virtue of our ordination we priests have an important sacramental and cultic role in the church. In the past there has been a tendency to suggest that the full significance of priesthood could be found in its cultic function. The post-Vatican II church has rightly insisted that the priesthood also includes very important prophetic, educational, social, and counseling tasks.

Nevertheless, the cultic function of the priest must not be belittled. The symbols, the rituals, the sacraments, and the liturgy of the church are entrusted to us in a very special way. When I preside at the eucharistic liturgy, when I baptize, when I anoint the sick, when I bless marriages, when I place ashes on the foreheads of the people at the beginning of Lent, on these and similar occasions I exercise the priesthood most visibly and most profoundly.

Third, by virtue of ordination priests are ecclesial persons, that is, we are authorized to act in the name of the church. There are, of course, other ecclesial persons. Among them are bishops, deacons, religious sisters, professed brothers, and monks.

But within this group the priest's place is especially visible and recognizable, for he is the one who is authorized and delegated by the church, by the community of believers, to preside at ecclesial liturgical gatherings, and to administer ecclesial sacraments, and to preach the ecclesial tradition. Although some other persons are authorized to do some of these same things, except for the bishop, the priest has the most comprehensive and unqualified authorization and delegation to act in the name of the church. And our exercise of this delegation is more familiar and frequent than the bishop's in the daily life of the church.

Fourth, by virtue of ordination priests are established in an especially close and publicly recognized relationship with other members of the church. Whether we like it or not, because we are priests, other members of the church feel that we belong to them in a special way, that we have a commitment to be interested in them and care for them. They feel that they have a claim on our time and energy, and if they are harshly rebuffed, they feel hurt and even betrayed.

Fifth and finally, by virtue of ordination priests are symbolic centers of the church, icons of the church, a sort of embodiment of the faith and the values and the traditions of the church. Certainly, the bishop is an even stronger symbolic center or icon of the church than the priest, and without doubt the president of the college of bishops, the bishop of Rome, is a still stronger symbolic center and more sacred icon of the church.

The fact remains, however, that when people meet a priest they feel that they meet the church and all that it stands for in a very special way. This is a precious and valuable asset, because it enables priests to have greater influence and effectiveness than they would on their own merits. It also carries a great risk, for it will inevitably magnify the opprobrium and stigma of their sins and failures.

These five closely related characteristics of the actual lives of priests are certainly necessary elements in any comprehensive treatment of the priesthood. But they are only five aspects of a very complex reality and I have not treated them in any depth. I know that I have left far more unsaid, unexplored, and undeveloped than I have actually expressed, but I am confident that further reflection on these five points can help us understand the priesthood better and exercise it more effectively in these changing times.

UNADDRESSED ISSUES

I would like to indicate very briefly two other items that affect the lives of priests quite powerfully and that I believe need to be addressed by the church in a new and creative way.

The first is the process of the selection of bishops. I do not hold a brief for a particular method of choosing bishops and definitely not for a popular election of bishops. But I do believe that the local church should have an open, clear, and effective role in the selection of its bishop. I also strongly believe that American bishops should be chosen by the American church in a well-defined manner and then confirmed by Rome, instead of chosen by Rome in a mysterious manner and only then accepted by an American diocese.

My suggestion is not prompted by an illusion that we will get better bishops in this way. In fact, my impression is that our bishops are generally above average in intelligence and talents, in integrity and dedication. My suggestion is prompted by a recognition of the increased importance today of the relationship between the bishop and priests.

My second item is the process of the recruitment and education of priests. I believe that we need to search for other ways of enabling persons to become priests, which would be alternatives to the present system. I do not argue for the abolishment of the process in which men make application to study for the priesthood and then, in the seminary, are given the theological, pastoral, and spiritual formation necessary for their future work. All of us were trained in that system, which has served the church fairly well since the Council of Trent. And I believe that our seminaries still give very good training to those who study in them.

But the present method of recruiting and training priests is obviously no longer meeting all of our needs. The continuing decline in the number of priests in the United States is reaching alarming levels. On the other hand, a continually increasing number of certified or commissioned lay pastoral ministers and of ordained deacons indicates that there is an ample supply of generous and dedicated leaders willing to serve the community in a variety of ways.

It seems to me that we ought to explore the possibility that dedicated and talented Christians who are already recognized as effective leaders within the church might be called to ordination so that we do not, in the words of Reverend Frank J. McNulty to John Paul II last September, "become only a church of the Word and lose our sacramental tradition."

Of course, many of the proven leaders in our church today are women and married men. Consequently, the questions of clerical celibacy and of the ordination of women come to the fore again.

Although premature and abrupt changes in those areas would probably cause more division and turmoil than improvement and advantage, it also seems quite clear, at least to me, that both of these issues will continue to haunt us until they are confronted realistically.

CONCLUSION

I realize that I have packed many undeveloped and controversial assertions into my reflection. But in essence I have suggested two theological principles that I feel should govern the development of a contemporary theology of the priesthood: first, that the ordained priesthood should be seen as the servant of the priesthood of the faithful; and second, that there is not a radical separation between the priesthood and the episcopacy.

I have further suggested five concrete characteristics of our priesthood as necessary ingredients of a theological reflection on the priesthood, namely, our presidential role, our cultic role, our role as ecclesial persons, our special relationship with other members of the church, and our role as symbolic centers or icons of the church. And finally, I have suggested two processes that I feel need to be addressed in a new and creative way: the process of the selection of bishops, and the process of recruiting and training future priests. Although I know that not everyone will find all of my reflections on these points sound or realistic, I do hope that they are at least thought-provoking.

EVOLUTION OF THE PRIESTHOOD
Adapting to Pastoral Needs

David N. Power

A changing priesthood has generated an interesting story about an unnamed parish in an unnamed country and the people's desire for good preaching. They sent their resident priest away for a year's study of the Scriptures, at their own expense, claiming that with the bishop's understanding they themselves could manage Sunday liturgies, baptisms, marriages, and funerals for the year. In the long term, however, they wanted a priest who could give them better guidance in the reading of God's word.

The story contrasts nicely with legislation, a thousand years old, that allowed a man to be ordained a priest, provided he knew enough Latin to read the Mass and could give a passable explanation of the Lord's Prayer and the Apostles' Creed.

Some things, of course, do not change. It is the nature of the things that the priest is busy about, and the way in which the Mass holds center place, that have changed.

Keeping the parish school going, serving the sodalities in the parish, conducting the novenas, hearing confessions were among the things that kept him busy in the fifties. Offering the sacrifice of the Mass day by day put him, however, in a holy space, from where he mediated things that the people could not touch and that justified his presence among them, however mediocre his preaching.

Today, the priest is more likely to spend his time with Bible study groups, with marriage preparation encounters, with the parish

social action committee, and with groups that are trying to address
such issues as drug addiction, the needs of the homeless, and neighborhood crime. The Mass serves to focus all of this in another way, a way
that gets the people involved in its preparation and celebration and that
leaves less tolerance for bad preaching.

CONSECRATED OR ORDAINED?

The language of the Second Vatican Council changed our way of
speaking of the rite of making bishops from consecration to ordination.
This reflected a more pastoral and less sacral conception of the office,
and gave importance in the ordination rite to the laying on of hands
over the anointing of the head. This is paralleled in priestly ordination
by the accentuating of the laying on of hands over the anointing of the
candidate's hands. The mission of ordination to the full ministry of
service to the church does not allow for the isolation of the Mass as a
sacred act that stands of itself. As an act celebrated with and for the
people, the Eucharist is the heart of a more complex ministry. The
removal of some of the aura of the holy from the office and person of
the priest probably has something to do with the decrease in priestly
vocations. It also goes with the increase of those who sense the responsibility for ministry and mission that runs through the whole body of
the faithful. The problem is not how to restore the aura of the holy to
the priest, but how to combine the provision of ordained ministers
with the collegial sense of responsibility that fosters other types of ministry and a more complete involvement of all the baptized in the life of
the parish, as well as beyond the parish.

RITUAL AND MINISTRY

There are those who think that the greatest change in the relation
between priest and people came about through the retention of Latin
as liturgical language when it was no longer the vernacular of the people. This was in sharp contrast with its original adoption for the precise
reason that it, rather than Greek, was the spoken language of Rome.
While a common language brings people together, the notion of language barrier bespeaks a real separation of life worlds. When the liturgy
became a ritual that could be heard but not understood, it readily

suggested a separate world into which the people could enter only through the mediation of one of the language's practitioners. The notion of a priestly office confided with distinctive sacred duties certainly did not arise with this, but it was greatly encouraged by the language barrier. The removal of the language barrier deprives the ritual of much of its force. If the force is to be recovered, it can only be through a better handling of the word by the presider. The movement of the ritual has to change accordingly, no longer suggesting the existence of a sacred space in which sacred acts are performed, but drawing attention to the holiness of God in the midst of a people who eat and drink at a common table around which they gather. In some respects, this is a less attractive and less comfortable holiness, one more easily tarnished because it is so inclusive and draws no spatial lines of separation between the holy and the ordinary. It is, however, if acknowledged, more evangelically powerful and more transformative of life.

A PROVIDENTIAL CHANGE

It is providential that this change in a sense of the holy, affecting the ministry of priests, should come about now. Europe and North America are no longer Christian cultures, in which church belonging is as natural as breathing air. A church and its priest at the center of a town or neighborhood could at one time symbolize the drawing power of the common recognition of God's name and mercy. Nowadays, the draw of the holy can come only through the testimony of those who gear their participation in society's concerns to the recognition and establishment of a divine justice. The retention of the divine name in the sanctuary hinders the establishment of divine justice in the town square and marketplace. Where the edicts of priests do not rule, the testimony of God's people may well prevail. They will not be wont to give it, however, unless the rituals of water and table allow them a full and responsible participation.

As we now watch the laity claim a greater role in the celebration of the sacraments, or witness the growing phenomenon of Sunday services celebrated without a priest, it is ironic to recall that priests themselves began to preside at Eucharist only in response to a need for an increased number of celebrations. The fact that even to this day the ordination rite speaks of presbyters rather than of priests is a reminder of it.

In early church order, the bishop was the one to preside at Eucharist, according to the principle of one faith, one assembly, one baptism, one Eucharist, one bishop. It was he too who taught the word. Presbyters were his companions and advisers, who shared responsibility with him for church governance and surrounded him at the celebration of the Eucharist, while deacons looked to the needs of the poor, the administration of church goods, and order in the assembly. It was when there were more communities than the bishop could serve in this way, that presbyters were sent to them for Sunday Eucharist, or that residents in villages and rural areas were ordained as presbyters, specifically to provide sacramental needs. In other words, when communities outnumbered the possibilities of ordinary eucharistic ministers (namely, bishops), a strategy was adopted that would provide regular eucharistic celebrations through the extension of the ministry of presbyters. In time, an ordination rite developed for presbyters that gave prominence to their eucharistic and sacramental ministry.

It took a longer time to recognize teaching as a regular part of a priest's ministry. For many centuries, in many places, priests were not allowed to do more than read homilies provided by bishops. These were not necessarily the homilies of the local bishop, but could be taken from collections of sermons by great preachers such as Augustine, John Chrysostom, Gregory the Great, or Pope Saint Leo. Catechesis often preceded liturgical preaching as a normal priestly responsibility. Such catechesis would comprise explanations of the Apostles' Creed, the Lord's Prayer, and the Ten Commandments or the seven capital sins. Explanation of the Scriptures remained the province of the bishop, or by way of exception that of gifted laypersons and priests who gained a certain universal recognition.

Throughout the centuries, the ministry of priests or presbyters has been tailored to provide what was needed among the Christian people to keep faith, moral life, and sacrament alive. However, since certain conditions of life, such as celibacy, and at times even membership in a community of priests, were deemed essential to good ministry, it has not been easy to multiply the number of ordained ministers in proportion to the number of parish communities needing ministers. Consequently, other measures have been adopted to provide catechetical and sacramental needs.

On the southern continents, in younger Christianities, catechists have kept village or station communities going, while priests visited them as often as possible for sacramental ministry. In more recent decades, priests have been less frenetic about rushing from station to station on Sundays to say Mass in as many localities as possible, since catechists and other local ministers have begun to conduct Sunday eucharistic services, as well as to provide for baptisms, marriages, and funerals. Since parts of North America and Europe have begun to experience a lack of resident parish clergy, the Sunday and liturgical pattern of life has begun to resemble that of younger Christianities. The relocation of the holy in the believing community and its action, rather than in the priestly act performed in its own sacred space, contributes to the possibilities of this kind of provision. If and when ordination policies change, as they have changed before, to allow all communities a fuller sacramental life, this will be done in a different climate, where the convergence of the ministry of all the baptized with priestly ministry is better appreciated.

In the meantime, the existing configuration of things is changing the demands on priests and the perception of their ministry. It is taking on more of an episcopal quality, with the expectation of better teaching and preaching, and with the requirement that priests encourage, supervise, and coordinate the growth of ministries among all church members. A good knowledge of Scripture and doctrine and good communication skills, both built on a foundation of faith in the church as the body of Christ and the dwelling place of the Spirit, are more and more essential to effective priestly ministry. Since the ministerial consciousness of the laity is much related to their awareness of being a people who bring God's presence and justice to society as a whole, it is next to impossible for a priest to function in the church today without having himself a strong sense of social justice and of the ministry of the church to the reign of God in the world. The preaching of the word and the coordination of ministries cannot be unrelated to this mission.

Knowledge of the Scriptures, theological education, communication and leadership skills, or the ability to promote justice, are by no means exclusive to the ordained. The priest may well find himself less equipped in each and all of these areas than some parishioners. But since bishop and presbyter are placed by ordination at the center of

church life, they have to be able to bring these skills together into a
single service of building up the church. Thus there is more talk nowadays of the collegiate quality of ordained ministry, or of teamwork
among priests. Apart from the fact that if priests cannot work together
they can hardly serve church unity, this emphasis on team ministry
reflects the differentiation of skills and responsibilities within a diocesan or national presbyterium, allowing for a divergent but convergent
distribution of roles among priests.

SACRAMENTAL MINISTRY

The one thing that remains distinctive of ordained ministry, and that
places the ordained at the center of church life in a presidential and
unifying role, is sacramental ministry. The church is always united as
one in the sacraments of Christ and draws its life from communion
with Christ in the mysteries celebrated. Whatever else bishops or
priests are ordained for, ordination to liturgical presidency is what gives
unity to all of their work and service. While the original presbyterate
centered more around the liturgical ministry of the bishop, ever since
presbyters began to be ordained specifically for sacrament the liturgical
presidency of priests provides the center point of their role in the
church, as it is the center point in the ministry of the bishop. The relation of church to society, however, and the nature of the relationship
between ordained and baptized in the church, point to different ways
in which this sacramental ministry has been or needs to be exercised.

Baptism, Eucharist, and penance have always served to identify
the nature of the church as the body of Christ. It is the nature of the
church's relation to society and culture that explains historical differences in the sense of its self-identity and in the pattern of its sacramental ministrations.

In his time, Saint Thomas Aquinas emphasized the power of the
priest to act in the person of Christ in celebrating the Mass and in
administering penance. His was a time when all human society was
deemed to be ordered in Christian faith and through Christian values,
in such a way as to mirror a divinely constituted order. Christ was at
the center of this ordered reality, and his restoration of an original
order disturbed by sin provided the pattern for human life in all its
relationships, as well as for sacramental participation. For Aquinas,

however, even more important was the ministry of the priest in confecting the sacrament of unity, in celebrating the sacrifice in which Christ's passion was commemorated, and in reordering what was disturbed by sin through the sacrament of Penance.

The model for the ordering of society was the reordering of sinful humanity by Christ through his sacrifice, and the satisfaction for sin which it rendered to an offended Father. Through the Mass celebrated by the priest, satisfaction continued to be offered in an act of homage, and through Penance, those who by sin had cut themselves off from the life of Christ's body were reintroduced to it by absolution, so that their acts of penance could be taken up into Christ's own satisfaction and gain value therefrom.

Growing practice exploited these theological insights in ways that Aquinas himself might not have countenanced in all respects, but that remain intelligible when seen in their relation to a Christian cultural matrix. The multiple offerings of the Mass for the living and the dead united the faithful on earth, in purgatory, and in heaven. A priest who heard confessions knew the penitent and could explore on the occasion of an annual confession whether or not she or he had been infected by heresies that drew people away from the true faith and from the body of Christ. A testing of faith and a service of unity in faith thus accompanied the conversion of morals and the engrafting into that satisfaction of Christ that restored divine justice and order, in the dispositions of divine mercy, and in the abundance of Christ's love. Within such a vision, a celebration of Mass or the baptism of a child or the hearing of a confession were very public acts. They contributed to the maintenance of a public order established on the basis of a common acknowledgment of Christ's name and a common conviction of the abundance of his redemption. If to us now there seems something limited or fallible in these perceptions, we are surely aware that this qualification is both invitation and caution to us in our own fallible efforts to embrace a mission to the redemption of the whole human order.

The medieval period of church life is one that continues to exercise a fascination for the Catholic mind, but we can escape this fascination somewhat by considering the place of church and priestly ministry at an earlier period when Christian faith was not the center of cultural life. A Saint Ignatius of Antioch or a Saint Cyprian could well see martyrdom as the principal service of a Christian to the divine claim on the world. A bishop's ministry could well be exercised from captivity or underground, and the capacity of the church to gather for sacrament curtailed on account of this peril. Penance was for those who tainted the body of the church, at times by their fear in failing to give public profession of faith. Penitents underwent long periods of conversion before being admitted again to the Communion table, which was the nourishment of the faithful and of martyrs. Bishops and priests were much engaged in the preparation of catechumens who would be strong enough in faith to join a community that witnessed to Christ's claims against pagan ones, and in the accompaniment of penitents who sought reconciliation with the church. The community's witness to the world and community sacrament were reciprocal to each other, and priestly ministry clearly served both.

TODAY'S SACRAMENTAL MINISTRY

These reflections highlight the symbolic and cultural aspects of sacrament and ministry. Christ's grace is bestowed and honor is rendered to God in sacrament, as faith teaches us. However, in the celebration of worship, word, prayer, and symbol allow people to see how grace gives them their Christian identity in such a way as to be able to develop appropriate attitudes to broader social issues. Today we face the crucial question about the place of the Christian churches in society. If the Christian community is not coterminous with society, how does it find its place as God's people in the world? Since this is a question of faith, it finds particularly sharp expression in the celebration of sacraments, and in the whole discipline and order of worship.

In inviting people to sacrament, in preparing them for it, and in presiding over its celebration, priests have to guide an expression of faith in sacrament which engenders an expression of faith in family and social life. All of the changes that have affected the life and mission of the church in recent decades come together in Mass and sacrament. Those who gather are more conscious of themselves as a body united in the Spirit and through the service of many ministries. They are also increasingly conscious of the fact that as a body they minister to God's presence and action in the world, and that this needs to be nourished through word and sacrament. While preaching and presiding, priests must surely be aware that attitudes to moral values and social issues will be educated and developed in the hearing of God's word and through a deepened understanding of the meaning of the sacramental rites and symbols through which Christ is present in the body of the faithful.

In short, today a priest will be able to give unity to all the activity of a community, and to the changing sense of the church's relation to society, if he is able to foster the awareness that the whole life of the church has its focus in the assembly of faith, where Christ and Spirit gather the faithful into one. None of the other activities that a priest now engages in will bear much fruit if the sacramental assembly is not a place where the Christian people can deepen their sense of being God's people, and their sense of the mission which they have as such a people in the society to which they belong. While a priest meets many other challenges, the one that remains at the heart of his ministry is celebrating well.

The power of good celebration has been greatly enhanced by the recovery of the scriptural word, especially of the Gospels, for Mass and sacrament. It is Christ whom the church remembers, into whom we are baptized, and around whose table we eat and drink of the gift of his Body and Blood. Since the liturgical cycle allows the priest to concentrate, with the community, on the individual Gospels, it offers him the possibility of recapturing the power and the faith of those presentations. This ecclesial memory is the antidote to the danger of an otherwise abstract sacramental celebration of Christ's mysteries.

Memory is not rooted only in a text but is inspired by life and its concerns. The memory of Christ's ministry, death, and resurrection converges with the Christian community's quest for life and with the testimony that it gives in the Spirit. Thus we come back, full circle, to the relation between priest and baptized as lived on a daily basis and manifested in sacrament. While recent church teaching insists on the difference between order and baptism, it continually speaks of priestly ministry as a service to the priesthood of the baptized. Priestly service empowers the baptized to discover the presence of Christ in their lives, to imitate him, and to testify to the reign of God in the midst of human doings.

Sacramental celebration is the action of a community of people who live their faith through the way in which they take their personal, family, and social responsibilities. They congregate out of a desire for God and a desire for a greater human good. The desire awakens to the memory that is preached and celebrated; it is formed and directed in its effort by this memory. It connects with the *agape* of the saving water and the Communion table, and becomes the heart of a common testimony and apostolate.

Many priests may feel they have already achieved a lot when they have found decent readers and musicians to enliven the Sunday Mass, and have convinced some parishioners to undertake preparation for marriage and for the baptism of their children. A vision of a priestly ministry in the midst of a priestly people and of a sacramental celebration rooted in an apostolic community can, however, stir a priest's imagination and give orientation to his interaction with people. This can be particularly effective in those situations where some are looking for ways to address the more compelling issues of modern life, where lives are being threatened and ruined. The priest cannot be expected to find answers to such problems by himself, but if he cannot speak well of God and of Christ, the people might well ask him to immerse himself further in the reading of the Scriptures and in prayer, while still keeping his heart attuned to human sufferings and to human joy.

MAKING PRIESTHOOD POSSIBLE
Who Does What and Why?

Michael J. Himes

Two issues must concern anyone who looks at ministry in the church in the United States today. The first is the need to encourage the emerging ministries of the laity. The second is the morale of ordained ministers, especially priests. The ministries of all the baptized are, in many instances, fledgling ministries. They do not have the clear definition of responsibilities that comes from canonical description and long-standing familiarity. All too often lay ministries are treated as useful and necessary stopgaps to which the church must resort because of insufficient ordinations to the priesthood. This implies that, were seminaries suddenly to find themselves deluged with applicants, lay ministries would fade away as no-longer-needed, extraordinary measures. The problem of morale among ordained ministers, on the other hand, has recently received a great deal of attention because of the report, "Reflections on the Morale of Priests," by the committee on priestly life and ministry of the National Conference of Catholic Bishops (see *Origins,* January 12, 1989). According to this report, many priests feel exhausted and discouraged because of the multiplicity of demands placed upon them.

RELATIONSHIP BETWEEN MINISTRIES

These two issues, the fostering of lay ministries and the reinvigoration of ordained ministry, raise two questions that must be examined: first, what is the relationship between ministries in general within the church and the specifically ordained ministries; and second, what are the relationships among the various ordained ministries, episcopacy, presbyterate, and diaconate? The answers to both questions hinge on an appreciation of the characteristic mark of the Catholic tradition within Christianity, the principle of sacramentality.

A sacrament cannot signify, cannot point at something, if the something is not there. But it only becomes there for you when it is pointed out. That is the peculiar sacramental causality that Thomas knew did not fit the usual meanings of *cause*. Sacraments presuppose the presence of grace in creation. They are the occasions for recognizing and celebrating what is always present but not always received. They make grace present for us by pointing to the grace that is omnipresent in creation. They make present and real for us what is always already there.

SACRAMENTAL CAUSALITY

The key to the sacramental principle is found in its classic form in a phrase that has its origin in Augustine's writings on sacramentality, and that was cited repeatedly by Thomas Aquinas whenever he turned his attention to questions about sacraments, namely, that "a sacrament effects what it signifies" (*Summa Theologiae* III, q.62, a.1). A sacrament causes something by designating it, by pointing to it. This can be understood only when an even deeper claim regarding grace is understood.

Grace is the self-gift of God outside the Trinity. If we accept that creation is a purely gratuitous and free act of God, that God does not need to create, then the only reason for anything other than God to exist at all is that God communicates God's self to it. To say that creation is a free divine act means that God needs to receive nothing from creation. The reason to create, then, is so that God may give something to creation. But anything other than God is creation. So the only gift that can be given to creation is God's self. The divine gift of self to creatures is what is meant by grace. Thus, the very ground of creation is the divine will to communicate the divine self. Creation is in light of grace. Everything that exists does so in order that God may enhance it. In a fine phrase of Karl Rahner's, grace is "at the roots of the world."

To say that a sacrament "causes grace" is, therefore, to speak of "causing" in a very particular sense. Thomas Aquinas recognized this clearly when he observed that sacramental causality fit none of the traditional meanings of "cause" that Aristotle had listed. This was why Thomas found the Augustinian tag that sacraments cause by signifying to be so useful. Grace, after all, has only one origin: the *agape* of God, the divine self-gift.

And grace is already given with existence, for existence is the first step in the process of the divine self-communication. Everything that comes into existence does so to be the recipient of the divine self-gift. What then does a sacrament do? It points us to the reality that is already present but not yet fully received. For there is in creation a point at which creation becomes conscious of the ground of its own existence and is free to accept or reject that ground: the human person. Those occasions—persons, actions, objects, events, places, times—which make us aware of the grace that is omnipresent in creation and in which we accept the divine self-giving are sacraments. The sacrament points to what is always there but not always attended to or received—grace.

All analogies limp, but perhaps a rather odd example may prove helpful. Imagine yourself in a dentist's waiting room. You are alone, waiting to be summoned to the dentist's chair in the next room. From that room next door comes the high-pitched whine of the dentist's drill, sending shivers down your spine. There is nothing in the waiting room to occupy your attention except the 1971 issues of *Better Homes and Gardens*, which seem to be *de rigueur* in all dentists' offices. In the background, Muzak is rum-tum-tumming mindlessly along. You pay no attention to the Muzak. Indeed, were you to leave the waiting room and were someone to ask whether any music had been playing, you would reply with perfect candor, "No, I didn't hear anything." Shortly, another prospective patient enters, sits down near you, and after a moment inquires of you, "What is the name of that tune?" At that instant, for the first time, the music goes on *for you*. That is how a sacrament causes by signifying.

ORDAINED MINISTRY IS SACRAMENTAL

In light of this sacramental principle, I maintain that all ordained ministry is sacramental. I do not mean that all ordained ministry consists in celebration or administration of the seven sacraments. That is obviously far too narrow a notion of ordained ministry. I mean that ordained ministry functions in accord with the sacramental principle. It makes effectively present for the community what is already there in the community, but which requires expression for it to be fully received and celebrated.

A fundamental shift is now under way in the understanding of the sacrament of baptism. Not very many years ago, were one to have asked the average Catholic in this country what the primary effect of baptism is, the reply almost certainly would have been that it removed original sin. That baptism is our admission into the community of believers would have been noted, but probably in the more individual-istic imagery of the baptized person's having become a "child of God and heir of the kingdom of heaven." In recent decades much more attention has been given to baptism as a sacrament of initiation. But all too often this initiation into the church is still envisioned as entitle-ment to benefits. The idea that by baptism we are commissioned to ministry receives far less attention. If mentioned at all, it may be con-nected with confirmation, a sacrament the theological understanding of which is far less developed than that of baptism. Baptism must be seen as the acceptance of a responsibility as much as the reception of a bless-ing. Like all the sacraments, it is received for the good of the commu-nity, not for the good of the recipient alone. One is baptized for the good of the others. That is why it is a public celebration of the church: it is for the church's good that this person be received as a new mem-ber. In all the sacraments, the common good is served equally with the individual's good. To be baptized is to be called into service.

As the introduction into a community in which all are called to service, baptism is the primary sacrament of ministry. All subsequent sacraments further specify the fundamental call to ministry extended in baptism. It is in this context that we can understand the claim that the ordained ministry sacramentalizes the ministry already present in the church. This is the background against which the relationship between ordained and nonordained ministries in the church is correctly addressed.

Not every action of a believer for others is describable as min-istry. In *Theology of Ministry* (New York: Paulist Press, 1983), Thomas O'Meara, O.P., has helpfully defined ministry as "the public activity of a baptized follower of Jesus Christ flowing from the Spirit's charism and an individual personality on behalf of a Christian community to witness to, serve, and realize the Kingdom of God." The public acts that witness to, serve, and realize the kingdom of God have differed and will differ from age to age and from place to place. The church is a multidimensional reality. As such, the tasks to which it is called and to which it calls its members vary with the historical and cultural conditions in which it lives. A ministry vital in one circumstance may legitimately disappear as unnecessary in another time and place. At any given moment in the community's life there is a multitude of ministries to which one or another is called by baptism and, in O'Meara's words, individual personality.

THREE RESPONSIBILITIES

But there are some responsibilities that confront the church always and everywhere because they are intrinsic to the baptized community. Corresponding to these responsibilities are forms of ministries whose relevance is never exhausted. The styles of these ministries may vary with time and place, but their fundamental natures remain. I suggest that there are at least three responsibilities that are present in the church in every age and on every level, whether in the church universal or the most local church, the family and household. They are, first, the responsibility to maintain communion within the church, the holding together of the community. The second is responsibility to and for the word of God. The third responsibility is that of direct service both to those within the community and those outside the community. The three forms of ministry that correspond to these responsibilities have traditionally been designated respectively as episcopate, presbyterate, and diaconate. By baptism every Christian is charged with all three of these responsibilities and so is called to all three of these ministries.

Catholics have long been accustomed to speak of a universal priesthood in the church, a priesthood of all the faithful. I am suggesting that, as there is a universal presbyterate, so too there are a universal episcopate and a universal diaconate in the church, an episcopate and diaconate of all the faithful. All are called to the episcopal function of maintaining the unity of the community. All are called to the presbyteral function of responsibility to and for the word. All are called to the diaconal function of direct service to those within and outside the community. The vocation to these universal ministries is given in baptism, which is the principal sacrament of ministry.

Because these needs and the ministries that respond to them are present at all times and on every level in the church and all are called to them, it is necessary that there be some who are asked by the community to sacramentalize these ministries. In accord with the sacramental principle that what is always and everywhere present must be embodied somewhere in order to be made effectively present, the universal episcopal, presbyteral, and diaconal ministries need sacramental expression. This is the role of ordained ministries.

When one is baptized, one does not receive a sacrament, one becomes a sacrament. Baptism makes us sacraments to the world, signifying and therefore making real the grace that lies at the roots of the world. Our baptismal second birth as Christians in the church is the sacramentalization of the divine self-gift, which is the reason for our first birth as human beings in the world. So, too, orders makes those members of the community called to ordination sacraments pointing to a reality already present throughout the whole church, and so rendering that reality effective. As sacraments, ordained ministers effect what they signify: the ministry of all the faithful.

Understanding ordained ministry sacramentally reverses a familiar but inadequate notion of the universal priesthood of all believers, namely, that the priesthood of the laity is a participation in the priesthood of the hierarchy. It is far truer, and far more coherent with our sacramental theology, to understand the priesthood of the ordained as the sacramentalization of the priesthood of the whole church. The priesthood of the church is primary. Its sacramental expression, ordained ministry, is built upon it, not the other way around. An important corollary of this should be noted. Central to any sacrament is the reinforcement of the reality that is sacramentalized. Thus it follows that crucial to a renewal of ordained priesthood in our time is a renewal of the priesthood of the whole church. Unless the priesthood of the laity is fostered, the priesthood of the ordained must languish.

Ordained ministers are designated by the community to embody a specific ministry, whether episcopacy, that is, the maintenance of communion, or of presbyterate, that is, responsibility to and for the word of God, or of diaconate, the direct service to those within and outside the community. Anyone who is ordained to sacramentalize one of those ministries is still called by baptism to the other two. When someone is ordained to the presbyterate, it does not mean he no longer has diaconal or episcopal responsibilities. Each member of the church has all three responsibilities by baptism. But now the one ordained is required to incarnate, to embody, to sacramentalize the presbyteral function specifically.

It is essential that the various responsibilities of these three sacramental ministries be sorted out. This raises the second question that needs to be addressed at the present moment, a question that has been largely unnoticed but that has extremely important consequences for ordained priestly ministry: what is the relationship among the three ordained ministries? The thesis I advance is that, for a very long time, the church has ordained people to the presbyterate but then charged them with the responsibilities of the episcopacy and the diaconate.

PRESBYTERATE OVEREXTENDED

The presbyterate has been a jack-of-all-trades ministry. A familiar phrase from Saint Paul has been wrenched out of context and badly misused, his claim to have become all things to all people (1 Cor 9:22). As a goal of service, that is admirable. As a job description, it is impossible. If one sets out to be everything to everyone, one will very quickly be nothing to anyone. The report of the NCCB committee on priestly life and ministry states: "For some recently ordained priests, the sense of professionalism and planning which they bring to ministry clashes with administration and service which they perceive as haphazard and without priorities. They find job descriptions such as 'all things to all people' or the priest is 'always on duty' as inept rather than impressive" ("Reflections on the Morale of Priests," *Origins,* January 12, 1989). The problem is by no means limited to those who have been recently ordained. The report further testifies to what was no secret: "burnout" among priests is a real and present problem:

> Role expectations among the clergy leave many feeling trapped, overworked, frustrated and with a sense of little or no time for themselves. The continuing shortage of clergy casts its shadow on both present ministry and future hopes. Official directives which focus on duties "only the priest can do" tend to increase the workload and make for less effective ministry. The lack of a unified, coherent vision of what we are all about is an additional burden for others. Perhaps underlying

all of this is a bone weariness of the spirit that has to do with
the times in which we live. It is a weariness that comes from
standing in the breach during a time of profound
transition in our culture and in the history of the church.

I suggest that many of the most talented and zealous priests burn
out, or, at least, feel themselves constantly under intense pressure
because the job description is so enormous and so amorphous that it is
clearly unrealizable. Many good priests go to bed every night feeling
guilty because they recognize that once again that day they have failed
to meet all the responsibilities which they assume and the community
tells them are theirs. That is frightfully demoralizing. Failure is
inevitable because the task is unperformable. Something is radically
wrong with the job description. What is wrong is that the episcopal,
presbyteral, and diaconal ministries have become confused.

What is the properly presbyteral role? Reference has several times
been made to "the ministry of responsibility to and for the word of
God." The word of God here does not only mean Scripture, although
Scripture is its preeminent instance. By the word of God I intend the
whole of the church's reflection upon and living out of God's self-communication. Thus what was classically called tradition in Catholic theology, as well as Scripture, is included in the word of God. This means
the church's praxis, not its intellectual life alone. The presbyteral ministry is that of *responsibility to* the word of God, reflecting on the
church's experience and action in light of the tradition, and *responsibility for* the word of God, reflecting on the tradition in view of contemporary experience and practice. It is a ministry of interpretation that
allows the tradition to illumine our experience and our experience to
yield new insight into the tradition.

ROOTS OF PRESBYTERATE

The presbyterate has its roots historically in the elders who governed
the synagogue. This connection between the presbyteral office and the
rabbinate helps to focus the priestly role today. As the rabbi's role is
above all to be the guardian and interpreter of the Jewish tradition, so
too the priest is the one who brings to bear the riches of the Christian
community's tradition on the present life of the church in order both
to shape that life and to enrich and expand the tradition.

This rabbinic role of interpretation of tradition and experience is carried on in many ways. Preaching, catechesis, counseling, spiritual direction, and liturgical celebration (since the word of God is proclaimed and interpreted not only in words) are all forms of presbyteral ministry. And it is precisely these activities that are often described as being in crisis today. Again and again complaints are heard about the sorry state of preaching in the church, about the need for more creative and authentic catechesis, about the lack of serious spiritual direction, about the dearth of effective celebrants of the liturgy. Certainly many exercise these functions besides priests. The presbyteral ministry is given to all the baptized. But the sacramental principle holds that a reality must be publicly expressed, that is, sacramentalized, if it is to be effective. Thus it is not surprising that the principal forms of presbyteral ministry are neglected or ineffective, when, at the same time, those ordained to sacramentalize the presbyteral ministry are frustrated by the confused state of their job description.

Priests who are pastors are performing episcopal functions. They are living out the classic episcopal model far more than bishops are or can today, because of the enormous size of dioceses in the United States and the complexity of their administration. Ambrose and Augustine, Basil and Gregory the Great would have been thunderstruck by the number of Christians included in a single one of our dioceses. By any realistic historical measurement, the pastor of a good-sized parish is far more directly the successor of the bishops of the patristic era than those ordained to the episcopal office today. Further, most priests are engaged in diaconal functions. Historically, the priesthood became a kind of generalized service: whatever needed to be done for the community or by the community for those outside it, the priest did. As bishops could no longer fulfill the episcopal role of maintaining the communion of believers one with another in the local church, and the unity of one local community with another and with the universal church, the priest as the local pastor began to do so. When the diaconate was reduced in practice to a step toward ordination to the presbyterate, it fell to the priest to perform the functions formerly given to the deacon. The episcopal, presbyteral, and diaconal offices are always and everywhere part of the church's life, and for that very reason require sacramentalization. When those ordained to sacramentalize the episcopal and diaconal offices effectively disappeared from the local church, the offices still required sacramental expression, and in practice if not in theory they have been transferred to the remaining ordained minister, the priest.

What has suffered is the sacramentalization of the specifically presbyteral function: responsibility to and for the word of God in worship and praxis, in counseling and spiritual direction, in preaching and teaching. Priests who are generous with time and energy, and who can truly say they have been constructively busy all week long, may find they have not been able to give ten minutes consideration to how the Sunday Eucharist should be celebrated or what they will preach from the Scripture texts of the day. And this is not because they lack zeal or are unconcerned about their pastoral responsibilities. The problem is not that they have not worked, but that quite probably what they have been working at are episcopal and diaconal tasks. They have not been engaged in the presbyterate, the office to which the church has ordained them.

The episcopal and diaconal responsibilities are as important to the church as the presbyteral. The ministries that correspond to them are as vital in the community's life as the presbyteral ministry. And it should not be forgotten that everyone ordained to sacramentalize the presbyteral ministry of the whole church has also been called to the universal episcopacy and diaconate by baptism, vocations in no way voided by the specific office to which he has been ordained. But the specific role the ordained priest has been charged with sacramentalizing is the presbyterate, the ministry of responsibility to and for the word of God. And it is that role and the duties connected with it that are most often slighted.

DIACONATE TOO PRESBYTERAL

The ordained diaconal ministry, revived in the last quarter of a century, has suffered greatly from formation programs and candidates unable to imagine any model for ordained ministry in the church other than priesthood. Many deacons devote much if not most of their time and energy to liturgical functions, preaching, catechesis for baptism or marriage, counseling, and so on, all of which are presbyteral functions. One can argue that these activities are the task of the universal presbyterate to which we are all called by baptism. But often the person ordained to the diaconate performs them. The ministry of service, including administration, which the deacon should sacramentalize, is far too often not part of the ordained deacon's job description at all.

A more serious danger is that priests who cling to the "jack-of-all-trades" notion of priestly ministry become frightened and embittered as they see others taking responsibilities previously the domain of the priest. And since virtually everything was formerly the domain of the priest, they can scarcely avoid seeing this as an encroachment. This leads to a defensive posture that somberly warns of a denigration of the priesthood whenever the ministries of the baptized are mentioned. As so often happens, a seriously flawed and thoroughly inadequate theological position portrays itself as traditional.

The most visible ordained ministry in the church, the priesthood, cannot be reorganized in a single sweep. The community is accustomed to expect that various tasks will be performed by priests, and it would be pastorally ineffective as well as unjust for priests to abruptly redefine their role in such a way as to disappoint these expectations. But the gradual shifting of expectations must begin. This will require priests, first, to appreciate their call to sacramentalize the priesthood of all the members of their congregations so that ordained ministry builds up universal ministry, and second, to distinguish presbyteral responsibilities from those that are properly episcopal and diaconal.

Theologically, such redefinition of the priesthood makes sense; practically, it is unavoidable. Whatever one may think of the church's ministries as we have known them, they cannot continue to function as they have. Church organization in this country and in this century (it has been different elsewhere and different here in an earlier time) has required large numbers of celibate men and women who are not available any longer. Reorganization is not only devoutly to be wished; it is inevitable. It is essential for the growth of lay ministries to which all are called by baptism. It is vital for the health of the ordained priesthood, which sacramentalizes the universal presbyterate of the church. The church has usually made the right decisions in its history, although often kicking and screaming when pressed to do so by circumstances. That is what is meant when we say that the Holy Spirit guides the church. Certainly it would be very pleasant if the community were to advance with courage and imagination. But one way or another, the Spirit still guides us, and circumstances are pressing.

THE PRACTICE OF PRIESTHOOD
Working Through Today's Tensions

James J. Bacik

During the past fifty years, societal, cultural, and religious factors have challenged the once-entrenched cultic model of priesthood. The cultic priest's main task was to provide the sacraments, most often Mass and confession. He led a distinctive lifestyle by remaining celibate, living in a rectory, and wearing clerical garb. Pastors worked as general practitioners, responsible for all aspects of parish life. Parishioners placed their pastor on a pedestal, as mediator between God and themselves. With the indelible character received at ordination, priests functioned as "other Christs," ruling and sanctifying the faithful. Most understood this role, enjoyed the respect of society, and found general satisfaction in their work.

Catholics, feeling like outsiders in a Protestant culture, relied on the strict authority structure within the church for identity and cohesion. After World War II, however, the situation began to change. Catholics gained advanced degrees, positions of power and influence, and affluence. They moved up socially and away from urban neighborhoods to the newly developing suburbs. The election of John F. Kennedy in 1960 signaled the arrival of Catholics into the mainstream of American life. Today, three-fourths of the Catholic community have "made it" socially and economically. Catholics rank among the most affluent citizens in the country. Even so, one-fourth of Catholics today, largely Hispanic immigrants, remain on the margins.

Such changes affected the cultic model of the priesthood. Large suburban parishes forced many pastors into a more collaborative style. Priests found themselves serving Catholics who no longer considered the parish the center of their social life. And laity made new demands, expecting priestly guidance in relating their faith to life in the changing world.

The Second Vatican Council intensified the pressures. The priest's new position facing the people during Mass symbolized a new relationship between pastors and parishioners. Many lay people heard rightly that, invested with baptismal rights and duties, they are co-responsible for the church. Consequently, they began to expect new ways of interacting with ordained leaders.

Today the church is still trying to understand the significance of Vatican II for parish life. One interpretation views the council as the culmination of the great liturgical, scriptural, ecumenical, and theological movements of the twentieth century. Thus, some Catholics, who accord the conciliar documents a fixed finality, seek to bring this era of change to a close.

Karl Rahner challenged this position by insisting that the council be viewed as the tiny beginning of a major movement in which the Catholic church would become, for the first time in its history, a truly world church (see "Basic Theological Interpretation of the Second Vatican Council," *Theological Investigations*, v. 20, pp. 77–89). In the future, Europe and the United States will no longer dominate Catholic self-understanding. New forms of indigenous Christianity will develop in Africa, Asia, and around the globe. Adherents of such an outlook think the current centralizing efforts of the Vatican are anachronistic and that one Code of Canon Law cannot govern a pluralistic world church. Greater liturgical adaptation is necessary for indigenous forms of Christianity to flourish. Rahner thought that the Vatican II documents serve best as a springboard for further reflection and adaptation.

Since Vatican II, the church has struggled to define the center of Catholic life and thought. There are competing views about what constitutes moderate or centrist Catholic positions. Liberal theologians stress the council's progressive spirit, claiming that the defeated minority at the council is still trying to resurrect its rejected positions as centrist teachings. Neoconservatives want their traditional agenda on center stage, while asserting that liberals are not faithful to the documents. The average priest in the United States feels the ramifications of these disputes in everyday parish life. Some parishioners, tired of changes, want more stability; others wonder when the parish is going to catch up with the modern world.

Tensions in the church have been exacerbated as well by the major cultural shift taking place as the world moves from the modern to the postmodern age. Modernity began with the rise of science and the age of discovery and found its unique voice in the eighteenth-century European Enlightenment, which insisted that science, reason, and democratic procedures would ensure human progress. Since World War I, that expectation has been challenged. Living in the wake of World War II, the Holocaust, Vietnam, Watergate, assassinations of world leaders, tribal wars, terrorism, and ethnic cleansing, it is difficult to sustain the optimism that characterized modernity. People know well the ambiguous results of scientific "progress" and technological reason, and the destructive effects of colonialism and patriarchy, key components of modernity.

Still, it is not clear what shape the postmodern world will take. One would hope that it retains the positive elements of modernity (freedom, democracy, and human rights) while overcoming the negatives (individualism, rationalism, scientism, colonialism, racism, and sexism).

Cultural shifting has brought a new set of complex tensions to the church and the priesthood. While traditionalists want to return to the premodern world with its authoritarian style, other Catholics want the church to continue its dialogue with the modern world initiated by the council's Pastoral Constitution. A small group of advanced thinkers insist that the church put its energy into shaping the postmodern world, lest the process be co-opted by secularists and/or fundamentalists.

Great cultural shifts raise radical questions about identity and meaning. Many professional groups in addition to clergy—doctors, lawyers, and teachers—are going through a period of self-examination. Men and women are searching for ways of relating to one other with equality and mutuality. Minorities want their voices heard. Heightened tensions are inevitable. Priests, as both participants in society and church leaders committed to compassionate service, experience these tensions acutely.

The challenge of our time is to make these tensions energizing and fruitful rather than debilitating. Can we find passion and excitement in helping to shape a new society and a new church? Can we summon courage in the midst of strife and chaos? Can we maintain hope when the future appears foreboding? Can we transform the inevitable tensions of being a priest today into a new energy for personal development and service on behalf of the kingdom? How?

One essential step is to make the tensions as intelligible as possible. By describing them accurately and by deepening our understanding of the dynamics at work behind the tensions, we can tap their latent power. The five specific tensions I discuss here are (1) theological, (2) personal, (3) relational, (4) cultural, and (5) ecclesial.

THEOLOGICAL TENSIONS

Fundamental theological tensions are built into the current understanding of priesthood. As we have seen, the cultic model does not adequately represent the experience of many priests today. A few years ago, commentators were predicting the gradual demise of this model as older priests retired and died. But now it is clear that many recently ordained priests favor the cultic model and have adopted the traditional clerical lifestyle. They see themselves as part of a separate clerical caste and resist the more collaborative approaches associated with the reforms of the Second Vatican Council. They generally espouse a traditional classical theology, which separates them from the priests who are more attuned to the pluralism of contemporary theology. Older priests, who have worked their way through the profound changes of the council, often find it unsettling to be confronted with a new version of a style and approach they left behind. Younger traditionalists often are not comfortable with clergy who have tried to adapt their ministry to the needs of the modern world. Unfortunately, these tensions can lead to serious polarization within a diocese and great stress and confusion within parishes.

Theological tensions are intensified because we have not yet achieved a common understanding of the proper shape of the new model for the priesthood, nor do we have a new compelling image of contemporary priestly life. Some stress the servant-leader model, which emphasizes the relationship between the ordained priest and the faith community. This approach, well summarized by Robert Schwartz in his book, *Servant Leaders of the People of God: An Ecclesial Spirituality for*

American Priests (Paulist, 1989), emphasizes that priests share the human condition with all of the baptized and participate in the office of Christ, the servant head of the church. It reflects the practice of priests who are intimately involved in the everyday life of people in the community they serve. The model is limited in its ability to encompass the experience of priests who are members of religious orders and those who are not serving in parishes.

Karl Rahner, a Jesuit well aware of such limitations, proposes instead a prophetic model of the priesthood, which puts the emphasis on proclaiming the word. This central task of preaching and teaching forms the basis for the responsibility of liturgical leadership and care for the needs of the people.

Avery Dulles has proposed a representational model (*Origins*, No. 20, 1990, p. 288) in which Christ is represented in the world by the church. The representational role is carried out by the ordained ministers, who are specially authorized to speak and act in the name of the Lord. Bishops possess the fullness of the priesthood of Christ, but priests are also configured to Christ by ordination so they can act in his person and function officially in the name of the church. This occurs especially in the sacramental ministry and in proclaiming the infallible teaching of the church. His model puts great emphasis on the personal holiness and deep prayer life of the priest, who must be constantly attempting to conform himself to Christ, the high priest. Dulles insists that priests are not sacred persons or exclusive mediators who exercise all the ministerial functions within a parish. But through ordination and the special character it imparts, priests are public persons, who carry a special weight when speaking in the name of the church.

None of these competing models has been able to capture the imagination of priests and laity or to gain total ascendance as the cultic model did in the past. In this time of great transition, it is unrealistic to expect to find a compelling model that will account for the diverse styles and approaches of priests today. We can attempt, however, to manage the resulting tensions in a more constructive fashion. It is crucial to promote dialogue between those espousing the contemporary models and those, both young and old, who find the cultic model congenial.

At a priest convocation in the Diocese of Toledo, a speaker suggested that each of us seek out another priest who held very different views and sit down and talk openly with him. I recall searching out a very conservative priest and discussing at length our various approaches to controversial questions, such as birth control. At a theoretical level, we had great differences of opinion, but when we talked about the practical ways that we tried to minister to people, we found ourselves much closer together, if not in total agreement. For me, the conversation was both enlightening and inspiring. It gave me a renewed sense that dialogue is possible, especially if based on a fundamental trust that others are at least as serious about personal holiness and serving others as we are. It is possible to respect the pastoral work done by another priest without accepting all of the theological assumptions undergirding it.

In searching for a new model for the priesthood today, one does well to recall the sage advice offered by the Dutch theologian Edward Schillebeeckx, O.P., many years ago when the question of priestly identity was emerging. He suggested that we not spend a lot of time and energy thinking about the uniqueness of the priesthood, but rather, put energy into serving our people. Applying his advice today, we need to concentrate on improving our ministry in a variety of ways: preaching better homilies; relating in healthier ways with people; and developing more effective strategies for peace and justice. It is possible to make this kind of effort even before there is a totally adequate theological framework for understanding it. Service can lead to satisfaction even without a compelling image of the priesthood attractive to all.

In order to manage fundamental theological tensions, we must not allow ourselves to feel like mere victims of large cultural and religious changes over which we have no control. The tensions can become fruitful if we see ours as a challenging period filled with opportunities to help shape a new and attractive image of the priesthood. In the effort, we can find inspiration in Jesus, the Suffering Servant, who labored tirelessly for the cause of God and humanity without seeing much success or receiving a great deal of affirmation.

Personal Tensions about Spirituality

Some tensions that priests experience today flow from the personal struggle to develop a spirituality reflecting Christian ideals and respecting the demands of active ministry. Concretely, how can priests balance a busy life of service with a regular nourishing prayer life? Traditionally, priests were formed in a monastic spirituality based on maintaining a regular regime of daily spiritual exercises, including Mass, the office, spiritual reading, meditation, examination of conscience, and Scripture reading. Some exemplary priests are faithful to such a regime and find that it enriches their ministerial activities. Others, despite good will and repeated effort, find they are just too busy to maintain these exercises daily. Failure to live up to a monastic ideal still advocated by official documents and important authors often produces either guilt feelings or a deep sense of spiritual inadequacy.

Some priests have developed a more radical and constructive solution to the problem. They have abandoned the frustrating effort to keep a monastic regime and concentrate on developing a type of situational spirituality in which their prayer and spiritual exercises flow organically out of their ministerial activities. For example, they say a quick prayer for guidance in difficult counseling situations, express gratitude to God when receiving an honest compliment, request the gift of patience in the midst of a boring meeting, or ask for forgiveness after being insensitive to someone in need. The principle can be extended to other spiritual exercises. Homily preparation provides a good opportunity for reflecting on the Scriptures. The responsibility for giving a talk can prompt spiritual reading around the topic. Stress and fatigue induced by ministerial activities can lead to adopting a regular physical exercise program. Driving to the hospital to visit the sick may set the stage for serious meditation. The key to such situational spirituality is to use events as catalysts for prayer and other spiritual exercises.

Traditional wisdom reminds us that this situational approach must be balanced by regularly structured spiritual exercises. Finding an appropriate and workable regular practice is a personal matter and cannot be dictated by monastic traditions. Options and alternate rhythms abound: daily Mass, frequent meditation, an afternoon of spiritual reading and reflection, a monthly day of prayerful goal-setting and systematic examination of conscience on past successes and failures. The choice of a regime should be based on two factors: that the regular exercise can be maintained even in the midst of a very busy schedule; that it have an inherent power to attune one to the workings of grace in one's daily round of service.

This whole approach involves the radical shift of making the situational primary and designing the structured elements around it. Busy priests who have adopted this method, often unconsciously, find it a viable alternative to the monastic approach. It transforms the inevitable tensions of a busy pastoral life into a fruitful means of spiritual growth. In working out this situational-structured spirituality, one would do well to reflect on the practice of Jesus as reflected in the Gospel of Luke, where prayer is so tightly woven into the ministry of the Master.

RELATIONAL TENSIONS

The working relationships built into ministerial service provide priests with some of their deepest joys and satisfactions but are also a source of stress and tension. Priests who have descended from the pedestal position implicit in the cultic model are struggling to find proper and healthy ways of relating to the laypeople they serve. The rediscovery of the traditional notion that priests share in the presbyterate of the diocese has prompted a re-examination of how priests relate to their bishops. Pastors of parishes have the difficult task of reconciling differences and promoting harmony among the various groups within a parish, including traditionalists, neoconservatives, liberals, radicals, and charismatics. Priests who minister to members of the gay community at times find themselves at odds with parishioners who have homophobic tendencies. The racial tensions so evident in society often demand the attention of ordained leaders of faith communities dedicated to peace and justice. Priests in the United States serve a Catholic community with sharp socio-economic divisions. Male priests are called upon to collaborate with and to serve women, who represent the wide range from radical feminists to reactionary traditionalists. Functioning as the ordained leader in a church with such diverse groups is a difficult and challenging task filled with unavoidable tensions.

In order to render these tensions more fruitful, we need a solid Christian anthropology that recognizes and celebrates the social dimension of human existence. All human beings are made in the image of God and stand as subjects before their Creator. This means not only that we are answerable to God, but also that we bear responsibility for other people. Together with all other subjects, we form one human family. We are interdependent beings. We must learn to see ourselves as integral parts of a single history and a unified world. Genuine freedom is achieved, not by distancing ourselves from others, but by participating in the life of the community, which nourishes and guides us. An anthropology rooted in the Bible insists that we humans are inspirited bodies, integrated wholes. Our bodies are not mere temporary receptacles for our souls. They are the real symbol of our spirit, the medium through which we interact with the world and other people. Our gender sexuality stamps our whole being and personality. Despite our differences, we human beings are living out one common story. We are empowered by a common Source beyond our control and are moving towards a Goal, which draws the whole human family into a final unity.

This social anthropology leads to an ethic of care and compassion for others. Ordained leaders in touch with their own spiritual depths know the joys and the sufferings of those they serve. The priestly task is to articulate the challenges and opportunities found in the common human adventure. The people served are not objects to be used but persons worthy of reverence and respect. The task of reconciling individuals and groups demands that priests deal honestly with real differences, while searching for common elements which bind people together.

This general challenge is well exemplified in the area of male-female relationships as priests collaborate with women in ministry and serve the diverse needs of men and women. The insights of the behavioral sciences can be a big help in this regard. To take just one example, Harvard professor Carol Gilligan, in her book, *In A Different Voice*, points out that in our culture, girls growing up bond with their mothers and thus develop an enduring desire for close personal relationships accompanied by fear of isolation and aloneness. On the other hand, boys disassociate themselves from their mothers, developing in the process a desire for autonomy and success, which is always shadowed by a fear of failure. Without going into the scholarly debates on this analysis, some priests have found that this simple insight helps them in understanding more about themselves and the women they work with and serve.

There is value in exploring this and other gender differences in greater depth. In the process it is vital that we respect the distinctive experiences of individual men and women. We must avoid stereotyping and forcing others into our preconceived notions. The Gospel of Luke is instructive also in this regard. It presents us with a Jesus who deals with men and women in an open and challenging way. Furthermore, it draws on the experiences of both men and women, Simeon and Anna, for instance, to illustrate important truths about the way God is active in history and exercises care for us. In similar fashion, the teaching and preaching of priests should reflect the distinctive experiences of both men and women, while keeping in mind the gender differences commonly recognized today. Practical guidance can be found in the large body of literature on feminine spirituality (e.g., *Transforming Grace,* by Anne Carr) as well as the initial efforts to articulate a distinctively masculine spirituality (e.g., *Wild Men, Warriors, and Kings,* by Patrick Arnold, as well as David Toolan's review in the Spring, 1993 issue of CHURCH).

All of the relational tensions experienced by priests involve a complex web of dynamic interactions. In order to make these tensions fruitful, it is crucial to understand the differences that divide as well as the common interests that unite individuals and groups.

One of the privileges of my ministry has been to act as a spiritual confidant for the peace activist and author Charles De Benedetti. We often discussed the significance of the agony in the garden for our own struggles with limitations and time constraints. One day his daughter called to tell me that her father was in the hospital, just diagnosed with a brain tumor. My mind reeled. This could not be. He had just received an $80,000 grant to study the history of the Vietnam protest movement. At age forty-four, he was in the prime of life. He had so much to give and to do. I went to the hospital to offer prayer and comfort, but once in his room I could only sob—no words emerged. Chuck put his arm around me and said, "Remember the agony in the garden." In the church community, we are all teachers and learners. We minister to one another. As clergy, we must learn to receive as well as to give. This perspective is vital in managing relational tensions. It takes on a deeper meaning as one meditates on Jesus the community builder, who knew the human heart and labored to establish a kingdom of peace and reconciliation.

SOCIETAL & CULTURAL TENSIONS

Many tensions in the priesthood today are rooted in the question, How should the Catholic church relate to our multi-faceted changing culture? Priests are leaders, not of a sect which withdraws from the world, but of a church which continuously interacts with society. Collectively, the bishops make many statements on public policy issues. Catholics struggle on a day-to-day basis to bring their faith to bear on their real lives in the world. As ordained leaders, priests are concerned not only with building up the body of Christ but also with extending the kingdom in the world.

Our culture is pluralistic, a product of diverse historical influences, including the strict ethics of Puritanism, the republicanism espoused by the Founding Fathers, the utilitarianism which became dominant in the nineteenth century, and the consumerism fostered by the mass media and the world of advertising in our own time. Society is plagued with a bewildering array of serious problems, including drug abuse, family breakdowns, urban decay, corporate crime, gang violence, and crime in the streets. The legalization of abortion provides a particularly vexing problem for Catholics today.

Historically, in assessing American culture Catholics have fallen into one of two polarized camps: those identified as Romanists, who condemned the culture as being too individualistic, materialistic and relativistic; and the so-called Americanists, who adopted a more favorable attitude toward the culture because of its freedom, tolerance, optimism, and democratic spirit.

Today, this distinction does not adequately represent the range of views in the Catholic church on the proper way to relate to the culture. Proposing a more nuanced analysis, Avery Dulles distinguishes traditionalists, such as James Hitchcock, who are highly critical of the dominant culture and want to restore authoritarian Catholicism to combat its evils; neoconservatives, represented by Michael Novak, who are very positive about democratic capitalism but insist that the Catholic church use its rich tradition to reform our moral-cultural life; liberals, such as Richard McBrien, who celebrate our participatory democracy and want to see more of it in the church; and, finally, radicals, represented by Daniel Berrigan, who are relentlessly counter-cultural and press the church to speak out against militarism, consumerism, racism, and the evils of capitalism (see "Catholicism and American Culture: The Uneasy Dialogue," *America*, January 27, 1990). Leaders of the Catholic community are bound to experience tensions in trying to hold together and reconcile such diverse viewpoints. The preaching and teaching task of relating the gospel to our culture is enormously difficult, especially when we consider its diversity and complexity.

Priests trying to meet this heavy responsibility will find valuable guidance in the great pastoral letters written by the United States bishops in the 1980s on peace and the economy. As church leaders and citizens, the bishops brought the church into the public debate on vital issues. They listened to diverse constituencies and gradually refined their position through successive drafts. They entered the debate as dialogue partners and not as authoritarian figures with all the answers. The pastoral letters offer a nuanced teaching by distinguishing universal principles acceptable to all people of good will; fundamental Christian teachings, which should be held by all members of the church; and concrete proposals which admit of differences of opinion among Catholics.

The bishops have indeed given us an excellent method for relating the wisdom of the Catholic tradition to important public issues. But we need courage to follow their lead and to address social and cultural concerns in our preaching and teaching. I am reminded of the example of Father Vaclav Maly, a leader of the Velvet Revolution in Czechoslovakia. Despite being arrested more than 250 times and severely brutalized on occasion by the Communist regime, Maly continued to proclaim the gospel and its liberating message. His advice to church leaders is to fight for the truth, to resist every temptation to compromise with evil, to refuse to be co-opted by societal pressures and to act courageously on our Christian convictions.

While preaching on social justice will not land most U.S. priests in jail, it could hurt the collection or alienate affluent friends. Courage takes many forms. The courageous pursuit of truth is an important ingredient in rendering societal tensions more fruitful.

Our courage is strengthened when we move beyond isolation to a sense of solidarity. In opposing destructive tendencies in the dominant culture, we can often align ourselves with others who have sensed the same danger. Priests who have fought hard against the excessive individualism rampant in our culture can find new enlightenment and energy in the emerging thought of communitarian thinkers such as Robert Bellah, Amitai Etzioni and Charles Taylor (see *The Spirit of Community*, Crown, 1993). The strategy of linking gospel values with constructive countercultural trends strengthens the effort to spread the kingdom in the world and reduces the stress of feeling isolated.

As we try to manage these societal and cultural tensions, we look to Christ the liberator, who preached the good news to the poor and courageously confronted the sins of the established leadership.

ECCLESIAL TENSIONS

Finally, priests today are forced to deal with many institutional or ecclesial tensions. Some feel the need to resist Vatican positions on mandatory celibacy, the ordination of women, birth control, and *in vitro* fertilization. Others find themselves in painful disagreements with official teachings on peace, the economy, capital punishment, and on some of the directions of the liturgical renewal. Individuals attempting to work out a new model of priesthood often feel the pressures of the hierarchy calling them back to the cultic mode. A shift in the apparent criteria for appointing bishops divides the clergy. The publication of the universal catechism has caused consternation among clergy who disagree with its tone, structure, and points of emphasis.

These large institutional problems appear to be intractable and the tensions associated with them inevitable. Many priests see them as the major source of the morale problem among the clergy today. It is important that priests remain involved in these great debates and not merely withdraw into the isolation of their own ministries. In doing so, some liberals find comfort in Karl Rahner's famous and influential teaching on the world church, which suggests that the church will gradually move away from centralized Vatican control toward great pluralism and flexibility in policy making. Whether optimistic or pessimistic on future trends, all Catholics can find some measure of hope in the traditional doctrine of indefectibility, which insists that the church, despite limitations, errors and sins, remains in union with Christ and continues to be guided by the Spirit toward its ultimate perfection.

It seems possible to discern clues and intimations of this ultimate victory in the life of the local church. The cause of renewal flourishes in many parishes throughout our country. Seldom, if ever, have we seen so many laypeople so actively involved in the life of the church. Vibrant inner-city parishes are ministering to the needs of the poor and are maintaining quality schools for the great benefit of minorities. Thriving suburban parishes have learned to meet the wide-ranging needs of their educated people. Large numbers of collegians enthusiastically attend Mass at Catholic centers on campuses throughout the country. Rural parishes often still function as the primary community for the parishioners. Signals of hope do indeed abound in the local church.

Priests often find that tensions over the great institutional problems become more manageable when they celebrate an inspiring liturgy
with their people, or enjoy the fruits of a successful Christian initiation
program, or observe parishioners living out the gospel in daily life.
Frustrations with institutional constraints do not keep us from visiting
the sick, feeding the hungry, preaching the good news, celebrating the
sacraments, providing Christian formation, comforting the dying, and
sharing in the joys of our people. It is in this type of genuine service
that priests find their identity and experience deep satisfaction. In turn,
these good moments can remind us of the importance of continuing to
work for church renewal so that the institution will be a better servant
of the gospel message.

CONCLUSION

The tensions built into priestly ministry are bound to intensify during
periods of momentous change. We can deal with them more constructively when we have a clear sense of the importance of our ministry.
We have the opportunity to be present to people during crucial
moments of their lives as they celebrate new life, seek forgiveness, reach
maturity, enter marriage, deal with suffering, and face death. We have
the truly challenging task of helping people apply their faith to their
daily lives and in turn, receive the great gift of serious conversation
with good people about matters of ultimate concern.
    Our culture needs precisely what the Catholic heritage has to
offer. Our tradition of community and our parish structure are vital
antidotes to rampant individualism. Our insistence on discipline and
simplicity of life counters the materialism and hedonism which
threaten the culture. Our understanding of sainthood is helpful in a
society whose heroes are less than exemplary. The Catholic imagination
has an appreciation of the mystery dimension of life, which challenges
the one-dimensional outlook of our secular world. Our insistence that
moral values are best grounded in religious convictions provides a useful antidote to the moral relativism which weakens society. We bring to
a world grown pessimistic about solving great problems an abiding
hope that history will reach its goal and that God will ultimately reconcile the human family. Priests are leaders in a community with a proud
heritage and a rich wisdom tradition grounded in the life and teaching

of Jesus Christ. We have the exciting challenge of bringing that wisdom to persons in need of a word from the Lord and to a culture in need of his guidance and inspiration.

A MINISTERIAL SPIRITUALITY
Reflections on Priesthood

George Niederauer

Should a priest be a spiritual leader? Yes, certainly! How is a priest a spiritual leader? That's a tougher question. In trying to answer it I will describe several situations that challenge the priest as spiritual leader in the Catholic community. Then I will attempt a profile of the American priest as spiritual leader, asking what he needs to be, to do, and to struggle with in order to meet those situations, daily, with grace, his whole life long. In these reflections I owe much to Robert Schwartz's book *Servant Leaders of the People of God: An Ecclesial Spirituality for American Priests* (Paulist, 1989).

By "spiritual leadership" I mean the prayer and service offered by Catholic Christians in the church, through which they collaborate in proclaiming and building up here on earth the kingdom of God in Christ. Given this definition, the vast majority of spiritual leaders within the church are not ordained. But the bishops of Vatican II insist on the intimate relationship between the priesthood of the faithful and the ministerial priesthood, even though these differ in essence and degree (*Lumen Gentium,* 10).

The priest as spiritual leader must follow the one Spirit, who leads by means of many gifts; indeed, the priest is most effective as a spiritual leader when he is most completely collaborative with the Spirit-led leadership of all the baptized.

A THEOLOGY OF PRIESTHOOD

Let me suggest the theology of ordained ministry described by Tom Rausch, S.J., in his article, "Forming Priests for Tomorrow's Church: The Coming Synod" (*America*, February 24, 1990): "The ministry of the one called 'priest' in the Catholic tradition consists of leadership in forming and nurturing the faith community, especially through a ministry of word and sacrament." Jesus Christ teaches that leaders lead by serving because "the Son of Man came not to be served but to serve and to give his life as a ransom for many" (Mt 20:28). It is easy to list the most predictable encounters in which a priest meets the people as a spiritual servant leader, giving a little or a lot of his life as a ransom for the many or the few or the one; the liturgies at which he presides; the homilies he preaches; the religious instruction he gives; the penitents he meets in the confessional; the people he joins, or perhaps leads, in prayer; those he meets in ecumenical dialogue; the patients he visits in the hospital or nursing home; the other priests, women, and men with whom he ministers; the people he meets in pastoral counseling and spiritual direction.

But the grace of spiritual leadership—and followership—meets the priest at almost every turn. Unpredictable persons and events challenge the ordained spiritual leader as much as any liturgy or counseling session. For example:

- the teenager who answers the door in the evening announces, "Father, there's a guy at the door and he looks kinda like a bum ..."

- some parishioners involved in Operation Rescue or in a group concerned about El Salvador invite him to join them in a demonstration next Saturday morning

- the six people at daily Mass begin the rosary together each morning the moment his foot hits the sacristy floor

- the Hispanic family comes to arrange a *Quinciniera* for their daughter or the Filipino couple comes to arrange the blessing of their new house

- someone (other than himself) talks too much at
  parish council meetings

- a parishioner invites him to a delicious dinner in a lovely
  home and then treats him to a collection of slightly
  nuanced racial, economic, and political prejudices

- other priests and lay friends discuss with him the
  bishop, the pastors, the provincial council, or even
  more elusive targets

In each of these situations the priest can be called to exercise
spiritual leadership, to respond to the Holy Spirit drawing him to put
another first, himself last, and Jesus the Lord at the center of it all.

TRAITS OF THE SPIRITUAL LEADER

What kind of person could possibly meet all those challenges well? The
Lord calls ordinary women and men to ministry, and across a lifetime
of prayer and service his grace makes them holier, better and better able
to give, receive, and share his love and peace and joy. So we need not
romanticize ordained ministry out of all possible reach or despair of
finding suitable candidates for it.

What qualities make a priest a good spiritual leader? Three church
documents, separated by nearly twenty centuries, give us remarkably
similar lists of traits to look for in an ordained spiritual leader. The lists
are remarkable for their concrete, practical, down-to-earth character.
They seem to have been compiled by people who knew from experience
what they wanted and didn't want in their spiritual leaders.

Paul sent the first of our lists to Timothy: "even-tempered, self-
controlled, modest, hospitable, not addicted to strong drink, not con-
tentious but gentle, men of peace, not lovers of money, serious,
straightforward, truthful" (1 Tm 3). It is not very abstract or pious-
sounding.

The second list comes from two documents of Vatican II, one
devoted to the ministry and life of priests, the other to priestly formation. Notice how little these expectations have changed in two millen-
nia: "goodness of heart, sincerity, strength and constancy of character,
zealous pursuit of justice, civility, fidelity to one's word, courtesy of

manner, restraint, and kindliness of speech" (*Presbyterorum Ordinis*, 3 and *Optatum Totius*, 11). But how does a priest get this way and stay this way?

SITTING ON THE PARK BENCH OF PRAYER

I offer four partial answers to that enormous question, answers I will examine a bit more closely later on. Consider these as brush strokes and necessarily incomplete as a profile.

The Lord calls a priest to prepare for spiritual leadership in the following principal ways: (1) by struggling to become and remain a disciple, involved in unceasing prayer and conversion; (2) by constantly viewing American and kingdom values alongside each other, in faith; (3) by pursuing a collaborative style of servant leadership; (4) by living creatively with the tension between his own frailty as an earthen vessel and his call to be a strong, radically Christian leader.

For the priest, as for any Christian, leadership demands "followership," that is, discipleship: a following of Jesus Christ, who is not safely dead, risen, ascended, remote, and out of the way of my will, my plans, and my opinions. Instead, I follow a Jesus Christ who is alive and well and active in the church. This church, of course, is full of my willing, planning, and opinionated brothers and sisters, in the midst of whom Jesus speaks to me, gives orders to me, and sometimes follows me.

Spiritual leadership is not primarily about accomplishing our goals; it is about doing God's will, doing it as Jesus did with love and peace and joy, always seeking and listening to the Father who sent him as a man for others. For this to happen the priest disciple must be involved unceasingly in prayer and the ongoing conversion that proceeds from prayer.

One might say, "Well of course priests must be prayerful!" No, not of course! Dean Alan Jones of Grace Episcopal Cathedral in San Francisco is fond of remarking that there are many ways of not taking a relationship with Jesus Christ seriously, and one of the subtlest and most effective is to go into full-time ministry. The effects of a lack of prayerfulness in the spiritual leader are soon evident. Quickly enough, the unprayerful disciple dwindles into a church worker: for the disciple, ministry is a labor of love, but for the church worker it is a love of labor, which given enough time and problems will shrivel and die, leaving burnout as its unwholesome residue.

Prayer is a struggle, and in our spiritual environment it is a countercultural activity. My own suspicion is that the story of the American Catholic struggle to pray can be called "A Tale of Two Benches." The two benches are the park bench and the bus bench. I go to the bus bench pragmatically, to get transportation to somewhere else; a successful visit to that bench is as brief as possible. While there I may restlessly crane my neck to see if that truck in the distance is really my bus; I may bring something to read, so I won't waste any time; I may remark to others waiting there that the service certainly isn't what it used to be.

The park bench is another matter. I go to the park bench just to go to the park bench. I may sit in silence with birds singing, children playing, and the sun shining through the leaves of the trees. Nothing is produced; nothing gets done.

My guess is that ninety percent of what we do consciously on any given day is bus bench activity. Prayer, however, is the quintessential park bench activity. When we inveterate bus benchers come to it, we can too easily arrive with our bus bench expectations; then frustration is a likely result. Over and over we must make the difficult but essential choice to let go of such expectations and let the Lord lead us to the park.

LIVING GOSPEL VALUES

The priest as spiritual leader needs more than prayer and conversion. With a prayerful and converted spirit, the priest needs to live the values of gospel and kingdom and to struggle against competing personal and societal values that would weaken those of the Lord. The spiritual leader is called constantly to hold local cultural values up to the light of the gospel; however, he or she must not drop out of the marketplace of American ideas and activities. This call points up the difference between separation from the world and separation from worldliness, a worldliness of spirit that results in what Schwartz has called "blurred vision, ambiguous decisions, inner confusion, fixation on false gods or inappropriate values, or perhaps no focus at all." It is easy for clergy to conduct their own lives and the life of the church according to the values of the marketplace, forgetful of what Jesus did when he found the tables in the Temple piled high with the wrong items. The radical attitude demanded here is not a mindless distrust of creation but a mindful examination of all values, assumptions, and choices in the light of the gospel.

Religious educators teach us the beatitudes of Jesus but our culture teaches us middle-class beatitudes such as these I have composed:

Blessed are those who own their own homes;

Blessed are those who go to college;

Blessed are those who can write their own ticket, are self-employed, keep getting better jobs, promotions, and more money;

Blessed are those who live on clean, well-lighted, safe streets;

Blessed are those who know the right people, have reservations, make wise investments, and can afford nice vacations;

Blessed are the winners;

Blessed are those who are alarming, clever, witty, and can handle people well;

Blessed are those who live in a place where the movies are first run, and change weekly;

Blessed are those who get waited on in a store, and don't have to wait on others themselves;

Blessed are those who can demand and get respect for who they are, and for what they say and do;

Blessed are the young, the strong, the healthy, and especially those who are sexually attractive to one another.

Woe to renters, the unemployed, drifters, oddballs, the sick, the old, and people who talk out loud to themselves on the bus—avoid them like the plague, because losing is catching!

Are all these desirable things evil? No. May we kingdom people ever allow any of them to become primary, central, or ultimate? No again. Comfort is nice, but it's not a gospel value.

So the priest as spiritual leader must be vigilant about values, but can be consoled and encouraged as well; he knows his own weakness, but also he knows the Lord's strength. This strength leads him to humble self-knowledge and confidence in the Spirit. Saint Augustine, inspired by the Spirit, spoke with the wisdom of experience, telling the wholesome truth that material goods, when we do not possess them, attract us, and when we do possess them, do not satisfy; spiritual goods, when we do not possess them, do not attract us, but when we possess them, they satisfy. The Bishop of Hippo is saying that the race between these two sets of values does not seem fair, but God has actually fixed it in our favor: the tortoise of kingdom love always defeats the hare of worldly selfishness, but only by staying in the race until the end.

HEEDING THE CALL TO LOVE

The call to Christian life and spiritual leadership, though, is only secondarily a call away from selfish values; primarily, it is a call to the love of God and our brothers and sisters. This is one of the sources of the modern mandate to practice collaborative ministry among all the people of God, ordained and nonordained alike. It is the third way the priest exercises spiritual leadership.

Reverend Philip J. Murnion has rightly said that "ordination is not a license for private practice." The priest as servant leader must not exercise a style of leadership which is unhealthfully fragmented and independent. All healthy Christian leadership is by nature interdependent. This realization, and the implementation of it in his ministry, will make the priest both holy and effective as a spiritual leader. It is the very "stuff" of his asceticism.

THE BATTLE AGAINST CLERICALISM

There is a world of difference between forming followers of Christ and forming a following for ourselves, and the name of that world is collaborative ministry. I suspect that the most pervasive danger to collaborative servant leadership by priests is clericalism in all its forms. By clericalism I mean the assumption (and the behavior which it produces) that the church functions mainly because of, and even for the benefit of, its priestly caste.

In the battle against clericalism it is helpful to think of Cardinal Mercier's remark to a group of seminarians on the eve of their ordination to priesthood: "Remember, gentlemen, God has called you to be priests because he could not trust you to be good laymen!"

I wish that remarkable churchman had been around to deal with a young, newly ordained priest from our seminary several years ago. Some months after his ordination I met a religious who was engaged in youth work with him. She had known him well before ordination, and afterward at a ministerial team meeting she presumed to address him by his first name. Whereupon he wheeled upon her and said, in front of the others, "Call me Father! I worked long and hard for that!"

I'm not so much interested in the rudeness of the "Call me Father!" part of it. What bothers me most is the bit about "I worked long and hard for that!" That smells to me of privatization of the priestly vocation, the noisome transformation of a call from God into some kind of ecclesiastical MBA. If a priest is called Father, it is for the same reason that he himself calls his parents Mom and Dad, and not Al and Edna: they are not better than he, but special for him, and in the way of loving servant leadership. We serve Christ in his people, and they have much to teach us about how to serve them best. We cannot learn it without humility.

The self-absorbed clericalist often shrivels into an empty, cynical sideliner, a belittling cleric who has quit but hasn't moved out; he needs our help but not our enabling.

Some lyrics of Stephen Sondheim illustrate this attitude for me. In his musical, *Company*, a tipsy upper-middle-class divorcée sings a song entitled "The Ladies Who Lunch." She proposes a toast to different types of suburban matrons, skewering each type along the way. Here are the lyrics she sings about her own type (I have substituted "priests" for "girls"):

> Here's to the priests who just watch—aren't they the best!
>
> When they get depressed
>
> It's a bottle of Scotch, and a little jest.
>
> Another chance to disapprove,
>
> Another brilliant zinger;
>
> Another reason not to move,
>
> Another vodka stinger.

ONE WHO HAS AUTHORITY

Even though the priest who embraces the collaborative model is gentle, humble, and cooperative, he is not a weakling or cipher. Holy people are not wimps! The avoidance of conflict is not the goal of ministry in Christ. People long for a priest to be a spiritual leader who will "speak as one having authority," a radically Christian witness. Catholics want priests capable of giving homilies with more substance and nutritional value than Jell-O left in the sun.

Priests are called to address community issues head-on, and not as vaguely worded examples. Bishop Untener of Saginaw has called for priests to "rid themselves of a caricature of their role as bland, colorless, safe, withdrawn, and secure."

The gospel has a radical quality to which priests witness: Jesus does not say "Go and put what you own in a blind trust and come, follow me," nor does he say "Let the one who hasn't sinned too terribly much recently cast the first stone." Accordingly, Jesus calls us to be radical in our witness and proclamation, but not to be strident. We can be patient and compassionate without being wishy-washy, and strong in faith without being narrow, doctrinaire, and judgmental.

A strain of inappropriate compromise in American moral and religious life flies the banner of realism. Preferring realism to idealism, we say to each other, "Oh, come on, be realistic!" But we seldom say, "Be idealistic!" Idealistic is not something to be—that is, unless you are a Christian, especially a Christian spiritual leader. Idealism gives us the courage to get misunderstood and laughed at for the Lord.

In practice the call of the priest to radically Christian leadership exists in tension with his constant sense of being an earthen vessel. One reality modifies the other; we are confident and hopeful because the Lord has chosen us as vessels of his saving work, but we are humble because of our fragile, vulnerable unworthiness. The misgivings, however, are no match for the hope. Once the priest as spiritual leader lets go of prideful perfectionism, he can hear more clearly the Lord calling him to meet those needs that he can (because he can't meet them all). He need not save everyone, or anyone, for the very good reason that it has already been done by an expert. This expert, the Galilean savior, asks for commitment and fidelity, not perfection and success.

THE WAY OF PERSEVERANCE

How do priests, or any spiritual leaders, persevere in the commitment to let the Lord keep making them over into good servant leaders? In this matter of our earthen nature, human fragility, and perfectionism, perhaps a helpful final image for the priest as spiritual leader may be that of a construction site.

Even though construction sites are signs of progress, they bother Americans. If you visit someone's home or rectory or church during remodeling you notice immediately the apologetic tone: "Well, you can't see it very well with everything a mess like this, but once the carpeting is down and the windows are in and all that stuff over there has been moved out...." All Christians, including priests and other spiritual leaders, are God's construction sites—in development, incomplete, messy, as life goes on. And for what it's worth, the church is a construction site too—the grandest and sometimes the messiest of all.

SURVIVAL MANUAL FOR PARISH PRIESTS

Neal E. Quartier

The U.S. Catholic Conference study, "The Catholic Priest in the U.S.," has projected that by 2005 the national priest-to-parishioner ratio will be one priest to every 2,200 parishioners, which is about twice what it was in 1975. It is a distressing statistic for the church in the United States, but it is mind-boggling for the parish priest.

The question the parish priest asks is, "How can one priest possibly minister effectively to 2,200 people?" The answer is obvious: he cannot. Unless vocational trends are reversed, the faithful cannot and will not know ministry in a way that meets their needs, at least ministry by priests as we understand priesthood today.

Consequently, there may be frustration and anger on the part of the laity, guilt and depression on the part of the priest. While not the only possible scenario, this is a plausible one. Even contemplating such a future is discouraging to those who might wish to serve the church community as a presbyter. It sets off a downward spiral: fewer priests leads to more work and frustration, which leads to even fewer priests.

Some Catholics speculate that a severe shortage of priests is the only way the church will change its policies on married and women clergy. This may or may not be true; without seeing into the future no one can know for certain. Meanwhile, what about those hard-working and dedicated men who serve now in parishes around the country and are already victims of this cycle of frustration? It could be that wrestling with demoralization and with an overwhelming ministerial charge is the sacrifice today's priests must make to live in an age of transition. Perhaps today's priests have to be men with courage to usher the church into a new age and to pay the price of such an enormous task.

If this is so, then let priests and Catholics admit it. Let's attune ourselves to the reality of the situation. Let us think and act creatively so that the priest today can be healthy and effective as he charts the waters of new and unknown seas.

It may be that recognition of the grim statistics on priestly vocations will give the church just cause to pronounce the passing of the present form of priesthood, to grieve, and then to let go of the priesthood that used to be. Meanwhile, the whole church must be willing to be creative and it must trust the Spirit to show priests ministering in this period of flux the best way of surviving.

If, however, the hierarchy and those in charge of priest personnel fail to acknowledge the reality of the current situation, one of two things will happen. Either more priests will leave or those who stay will have to struggle on their own to survive.

It is possible that some priests who choose to remain in ministry will not bother to fight the surface issues, but will look for alternative ways to build up their flagging self-esteem. The priesthood would still be important to them, but they would find self-affirmation and value in pursuing a second profession to complement priesthood, such as law, psychology, or education. Subsequently, priesthood would no longer be the center of their lives.

Other priests may find themselves involved compulsively in a number of activities. Although the priesthood fails to give such priests the self-esteem they need, they are unable to find it in any healthy ways. They become over-busy.

Of course, there will be a number of very dedicated men who will continue to struggle to keep the priesthood as they know it alive. They may even be quite effective in their work. Yet, it seems that there are fewer and fewer of such priests in parish life.

Catholics cannot afford to "do nothing and simply hope for the best." Even if the bishops are unable to deal with the long-range issues (which many Catholics see as the ordination of married men and/or women clergy), they must still deal with the experience of the priest today. Priestly ranks are getting smaller and many in the ranks are getting angrier and wearier.

As priests, we need to admit openly our common burden and work together to create a manual for survival until the church is ready to make some serious and far-reaching decisions. The survival manual must admit the gravity of the "vocation crisis": that praying for vocations, even increasing vocations by twenty-five percent, would not remedy the problem.

Today's priests can survive this era of transition and minister effectively through it all. To assist that transition, here are descriptions of ten chapters of a parish priest's survival manual that needs to be written and heeded.

SURVIVAL MANUAL FOR PARISH PRIESTS

Chapter One: Lay Involvement

The shortage of priests and the changing form of priesthood is a struggle that involves the entire church, not merely priests and bishops. The laity need to play a major role in guiding the church through the crisis. The laity need and want to share the burden for shaping the priesthood of the future. Therefore, it is important for the church to encourage the theological training of laity through formal seminary programs and through diocesan ministry formation programs that provide them with the tools and developmental skills they need to be leaders in a changing church.

Chapter Two: Expectations of Chancery and Congregation

One of the most frustrating experiences for priests today is that, despite the clergy shortage, there is no shortage of expectations. As much is expected of them as was expected of priests in the 1950s, when other priests supported them and shared the work. In the modern diocese, chancery mailings to parishes never stop demanding all kinds of programs and money. People in the pews still expect the priest to attend every committee meeting and event, as well as to counsel those who drop by, to preach well, and to visit grandmother and other loved ones in the hospital—all between weddings and funerals, of course.

The 1950s are over and both chancery and congregation need to accept this fact. Because the idealized version of a priest—someone resembling Bing Crosby's character in *The Bells of St. Mary's*—is mistaken as the norm, it is difficult for many to accept the limits of contemporary priests. Whether unfortunately or fortunately, such an ideal priest can almost never be found. Priests themselves will have to educate the hierarchy and the people realistic expectations. They may even have to help parishioners grieve the loss of available clergy.

Chapter Three: Talents

Not all priests have the same talents and abilities. While basic preaching skills can be learned, for example, all priests will not be equally good at preaching. Some priests are better administrators, counselors, teachers, or confessors. Priests themselves need to recognize and accept these differences. Others can assist them by encouraging their talents while also accepting their limitations.

An effective evaluation tool to help presbyters recognize their talents and weak points would be of great help in matching individual priests with the needs of a particular parish. This might prevent many frustrations and dashed expectations from both priest and parish. It might also allow a priest who recognizes a personal limitation to find creative ways to enlist others more qualified to perform specific tasks of administration or counseling or preaching as needed. It is unrealistic and destructive for Catholics to expect every priest to be a Fulton Sheen, or to cover responsibilities that a team of priests covered in earlier days.

Chapter Four: Personnel Policies

As all priests are not administrators or preachers, neither are all priests at their best in a parish setting. This is difficult to admit because it seems fundamental that the diocesan priest is ordained for the parish. Although it may be the ideal, it is neither real nor practical. Both priests and parishioners are aggravated when priests are forced to work in parishes when their particular strengths and talents lie in other ministries. Parishes can be harmed when personnel holes are filled by priests with little or no desire or talent for parish work.

It would also hurt dioceses and religious orders to limit sabbaticals and further studies for priests, or to delay a priest's retirement. The shortage of priests is not an adequate rationale.

It may also prove destructive to put one priest in charge of many parishes. True, it is unfortunate if some parishes are without a resident priest or have to close. The church needs to create a just procedure for determining which parishes cannot be filled, and which must close or be combined with other parishes. Such a procedure will be complicated; it calls for utmost sensitivity.

Chapter Five: Living Situation and Salary Structure

One of the loneliest places in the world can be a parish rectory, and it will get lonelier as the numbers of clergy dwindle. To force men to live alone in big houses, if they find that personally difficult, can be self-defeating. Options should be available for priests to create comfortable living situations with one another. Some priests may choose to live with a group. Others may wish to live alone.

Priests should receive an adequate salary so they can purchase or rent private living quarters and provide for themselves the cooking and housekeeping services that were formerly provided in rectories (and kept many priests dependent and adolescent). In modern society, independence is valued and self-worth is judged by the salary one makes. Of course the church is witness against any shallow understanding of independence, and against the idea that one's earnings define oneself. Still, like everyone else, priests are affected by these societal values. Paying the priest a salary adequate to make him responsible for himself does not necessarily erode the gospel message. It could make the gospel even more significant and real, and the priest more empathetic with the struggles of others.

Chapter Six: Professional Competence

In order for priests to maintain their self-esteem in today's period of transition, opportunities for continuing theological education are important. The clergy need to be open to learning new skills and to taking up new areas of study. Priests should be strongly encouraged to attend workshops, courses, retreats, and to take sabbaticals in settings where some updating can occur. They should also be encouraged to pursue additional degrees in theology and related fields.

Sometimes dioceses are overly cautious about higher education, as if a degree encourages a priest to leave the priesthood. If that happens in a given case, it must be seen as positive. As a rule, however, parishes and dioceses will have to become more open to priests working in fields related to theology, or working in parishes part-time and part-time in related fields. Enhanced professional competence can uplift a priest's self-esteem and be a genuine service to the church.

Chapter Seven: Deacons and Women Religious

Too often clergy see themselves as locked in competition with deacons and women religious. Since both groups are a vital part of the church and both are affected by the shortage of vocations to the priesthood, priests must allow deacons and women religious to be a core part of the current struggle. For example, the clergy would do well to listen to their input on diocesan restructuring. In parish life and in diocesan administration, deacons and women religious may already be prepared to assume the roles formerly held by priests that are open to them at this point in history.

Chapter Eight: Cooperation among Clergy

Neither the priest nor the parish can be all things to all people. The parish is the center of worship and the priest is the leader of that worship. The priest brings the community together and sends them out on mission. The central role of the parish and the central role of the priest need to be clear. All else is secondary and flows from these. The people must understand these respective roles. Priests in a local area or region should plan to stagger parish Mass schedules, to cover for one another, to cooperate rather than to compete with one another. Pastors can no longer be concerned about losing money or parishioners because the parish does not offer the earliest Mass in the neighborhood.

Chapter Nine: Acceptance of Candidates

Even though the priest shortage is problematic, or precisely because it is, the church ought to be more selective rather than more lax about candidates for ordination. Those ordained will need to be healthy, flexible, spiritual, and whole. It seems there are many dysfunctional people applying for priesthood today. The temptation to ordain any man who has an interest in the priesthood is understandable but dangerous. Ordaining fewer priests is preferable to ordaining more spiritually or emotionally immature priests.

Chapter Ten: Personal Life

Finally, each priest must accept responsibility for being as healthy physically, emotionally, spiritually, and psychologically as he can be. This involves his relationship with God, and with other men and women. Because each priest knows his particular weaknesses and strengths, he is ultimately responsible for offering to the people of God a holy and healthy priest. This cannot be done in isolation or without input from others.

CONCLUSION

Upon these ten suggestions a survival manual for priests might be constructed, not literally but figuratively. Such a manual would be created cooperatively, by those affected. It should be developed from a posture of acceptance and realism, not from defensiveness. A guidebook of this kind could come only from a church that has decided to abandon rigidity and from a presbyterate committed to change. It is a handbook that could come from a presbyterate open to the Spirit working in these "in-between times" and willing to become, as John the Baptist, one who prepares the way.

TAKING RESPONSIBILITY FOR HOPE
One Priest's Prescription

Thomas J. Morgan

Priests sometimes appear in the media these days as interesting subjects for TV and radio talk shows. It's not surprising since priests continue to be very important and essential in the lives of many people. Most are surprised when priests fail to live up to the high ideals set for them, an expectation illustrating that priests are among the few public figures still held accountable for their actions.

Millions of people, their hearts restless for spiritual values, continue to seek the presence of a priest, hoping to encounter the divine in his life. They look for priests who are models of Christian spirituality, wise men who immerse themselves in prayer, reflection, and meditation, and who periodically rest and renew themselves. Priests are invited to celebrate other people's most important moments, moments of suffering and joy, despair and hope. When people look for God, they often look to priests as well.

Many priests are themselves also on a quest for deeper meaning. They seek to live lives grounded in faith and conviction, believing that who they are as priests makes a difference to others. Some priests say they are not getting what they want out of ministry, that they want lives more prayerful, more God-centered. They seek the fruits of prayer: joy and a deeper capacity for compassion and trust, satisfaction and acceptance. Many also want to be more at home with their sexuality and masculinity and in general, many priests seek less stress and hassle.

Not surprisingly, the priest's self-confidence, so critical to strong leadership, is often jolted by media attacks on the credibility and identity of clergy in general. Some priests become confused not only about their priorities but about what is right and wrong. They may develop habits—such as smoking, drinking, or overworking—that they want to overcome. They may still enjoy the social status of priesthood, yet their work is less fulfilling. Priests are vulnerable to the negative judgments of those they serve. Disenchantment may set in; they feel blocked and limited as they face extraordinary demands, including the need to be refreshed and renewed.

Aware of the spiritual needs and longings of priests, the Second Vatican Council charged bishops to "exercise the greatest care in the progressive formation of the diocesan body of priests" (*Decree on the Ministry and Life of Priests,* 7). The following reflections on priestly morale include four concrete ways to boost it.

LOW MORALE

We are still facing a morale crisis in the church. The U.S. Bishops Committee on Priestly Life and Ministry, in its document *Reflections on the Morale of Priests* (1989), has defined morale as "an internal state of mind with regard to hope and confidence." The bishops see morale as a beneath-the-surface issue, affecting priests spiritually, emotionally, and physically. Morale is also a powerful determinant of how a priest may act in relationship to himself and the outside world of ministry and service. When the morale of priests is low, the quality of ecclesial life diminishes and almost every area of church life suffers, from evangelization to vocations, from liturgical celebration to service with and to the people of God.

A major factor behind low morale is a negative, erroneous perception of the priest as one who has no control over his own life and who is impotent before the major events and directions of life. Low morale prevents high performance, thwarts a deep sense of joy and fulfillment in ministry, and prevents growth in commitment.

Psychiatrist James J. Gill has described priests who have struggled with commitment and left the priesthood as virtually all being depressed, with personalities that are "perfectionistic, task-oriented, and aiming unconsciously at recognition and approval from those they serve" (*Medical Insight,* 1969). As Gill writes, they lack self-esteem.

More often, though, depression and low self-esteem among the clergy are described in the journals as low morale. Low morale expresses itself as unworthiness, unhappiness, unfulfillment, and anger. Thomas B. Drummon, writing in the newsletter of The New Life Center (Winter 1995), echoes the observation, "The number of clerics and religious who live in anger because they feel they are unaffirmed by authority figures is remarkable."

Some priests live in anger and shame, believing themselves unworthy of respect and reverence. By devaluing themselves, they find it hard to experience meaning in the priesthood. They may even begin to wonder if life is worth living. Ultimately they may become ineffective and isolated, unable to imagine possibilities for the future. Lacking a sense of vision and mission, they feel far from God. Unable to honor the God within, they cannot honor the God in others. Nor can they proclaim God's word with meaning and conviction.

Depression, Freud wrote, is anger turned inward. In keeping with that view, many therapists urge depressed patients to get in touch with their anger and to express it constructively without poisoning their relationships with others. Low morale cripples our ability to tap our intuitive inner wisdom and guidance for the daily task of ministry. It may also leak out to those we serve; despite our use of the right words, we may actually be communicating something else: our own low morale and hopelessness.

The bishops' document on priestly morale implies that low morale is a serious and substantial problem, one the individual priest must inoculate himself against. How, exactly? By (1) taking responsibility for his life and vocation; (2) promoting his own self-confidence; and (3) working heroically on being hopeful.

1. Taking Responsibility

Taking responsibility means that the individual priest is accountable to God, himself, and others for the quality of his spiritual, emotional, and physical life. He is responsible for it because he has the call and commitment to nurture it. He is accountable for the decisions, priorities, and actions in his life because he has the capacity to control and direct them.

Taking responsibility for one's growth and development is healthy and life-giving. It demonstrates an active (vs. passive) orientation to one's self and ministry. Self-responsibility also determines, to a large extent, the degree of growth, satisfaction, and success one makes in all areas of life.

Pope John Paul II, addressing seminarians and priests (*Pastores Dabo Vobis*, VI, 7O), writes: "We must not forget that the candidate himself is a necessary and irreplaceable agent in his own formation. All formation, priestly formation included, is ultimately a self-formation. No one can replace us in the responsible freedom that we have as individual persons." By taking responsibility one becomes part of the solution, not part of the problem. When I take responsibility I begin to work on my own distorted thinking and feeling, over which I have control.

Taking ownership for our morale as priests is an integral part of ongoing formation. It means that, regardless of past experiences or present circumstances, we "own" what we are feeling now; it is "ours" and we have to take care of it. Conversely, denial is one of the great ways we refuse to take responsibility for our thoughts, feelings, and actions. Denial leads to hiding from ourselves; it keeps us fragmented and afraid. As priests, we cannot spend our time naming and blaming. Taking responsibility for our own spiritual journey implies respecting other peoples' rights and recognizing that others do not exist simply to satisfy our needs.

No bishop, major superior, spiritual director, or counselor can give or take away our high or low morale. "It is the priest himself who is primarily responsible for ongoing formation" (*Directory for the Life and Ministry of Priests*, Congregation for the Clergy, 1994).

We must work hard at undoing the mental habits that contribute to low morale and challenge any negative self-talk that may be lurking beneath the surface to reclaim and reshape the way we look at ourselves and others. "Truly each priest has the duty, rooted in the sacrament of holy orders, to be faithful to the gift God has given him and to respond to the call for daily conversion which comes with the gift itself" (*PDV,* 79).

As a very young priest, Saint Gregory Nazianzus, in a moment of reflection and enlightenment on the need for responsibility for self, exclaimed that "we must begin by purifying ourselves before we purify others; we must be instructed to be able to instruct others; we must become light to illuminate others; we must draw close to God to bring God close to others; we must be sanctified to sanctify and lead by the hand and counsel prudently" (*Catechism of the Catholic Church,* 397).

The spiritually mature priest accepts personal responsibility for his own life and morale, which is rooted in confidence and hope.

2. Self-Acceptance and Self-Confidence

Self-acceptance allows us to integrate our strengths and weaknesses, using the power of our "dark side" for growth and development. Self-acceptance is the beginning of the spiritual search for meaning and con-nectedness with self and others. Self-accepting priests refuse to measure their intrinsic worth by their extrinsic achievements or by what others think of them. They avoid rating themselves. They enjoy being alone with themselves. The task of self-acceptance is a noble and lifelong process, and a key element in the dynamic process of self-confidence.

Self-confidence arises from knowing ourselves and being coura-geous enough to accept ourselves as we are—with our particular strengths and weaknesses. Self-confidence is crucial in the priest's life and ministry, for it touches on his ability to create within himself a quiet place where God speaks. It involves his ability to give and receive support and love.

Cardinal Suenens describes the model of church leadership for our times when he said, "The leader is no longer the man who has all the answers but the man who succeeds in creating the environment in which dialogue, research, and constructive criticism are possible and in which the answers emerge by the gradual process of consent."

A healthy self-confidence, rooted in the belief that I am unique and precious in the eyes of an infinitely loving God, can promote dia-logue, for it is rooted enough to be open to constructive criticism. Grace, which builds on nature, promotes self-knowledge, self-accept-ance, and self-confidence. In order that his ministry may be humanly as credible and acceptable as possible, it is important that the priest should mold his human personality in such a way that it becomes a bridge and not an obstacle for others in their meeting with Jesus Christ the redeemer of man (*PDV,* 43).

The priest must uncover what has created his self-doubts and insecurities and begin to liberate himself from them. He will find beneath his fears his true self, which is a temple of God's Spirit. This is the source of genuine self-confidence necessary to ministry.

Self-confidence is born out of the belief that I am capable of living and ministering as a priest because I "can do all things through Him who strengthens me." What a solid spiritual foundation for believing in oneself! The center of my being is essentially good because Christ redeemed me, is formed in me, and will abide in me until the end of time. This deep awareness of who we are as redeemed by the blood of Jesus promotes happiness, health, and holiness. It becomes the lens through which the priest sees his ministry.

Thomas Moore, in *Care of the Soul,* concludes his chapter on love with this reflection: "There is no way toward divine love except through the discovery of human intimacy and community. One feeds on the other." Self-knowledge and self-acceptance become the doorway to an experience of the infinite love of God. Love of self and love of God feed on each other. To act *"in persona Christi"* is to live one's vocation with intense self-confidence.

3. Hope

Hope is being deeply convinced that through the mystery of our union with Christ and the empowerment that flows from it God's caring love and mercy will continue in the present and in the future. "We have a sure hope and the promise of an inheritance that can never be spoiled or soiled and never fade away" (1 Pt 1:4). Hope keeps us going in spite of doubt, fear, danger, or bad news. Like Job, who lost fame and gain and heard voices of despair and doom, the priest is called to trust in the Lord. Like Job he waits for God to illumine his darkness. Like Job he is called to look beyond the surface and look hopefully to the future while in the midst of trials, sufferings, confusions, and questions. Like Job the priest must believe that God can transcend human reason.

Parishioners have a propensity to imitate the behavior of their spiritual leaders, so the priest who models hope can be a great source of comfort and consolation. "A priest, because of the Person he represents and the message he brings, is one whose ministry is expected to bring joy, consolation and hope" (*Called To Serve, Called To Lead,* p.18). But I can only model hope if I deeply believe that God offers unconditional love and will not abandon us.

"All my hope, O Lord, is in your loving kindness" (Ps 13:4) writes the psalmist. The hope grounded in the love of God becomes foundational for all our lives and ministries. It expresses itself as kindness and gentleness; as understanding and forgiveness; as collaboration and patience; as trust and loyalty; as joy and cheer; as commitment and fidelity; and as integrity and honesty. It allows us to see that we can become more than we currently are because we now bear in our hearts the love of God for us. As Saint Paul has written, "We walk by faith and not by sight" (2 Cor 5:6).

CONCLUSION

Priests with high morale tend to live and work with a healthy self-confidence and a joyful hope for the future, accepting responsibility for their own lives rather than blaming others. They don't need to hold others—especially authority figures—responsible for their own feelings, thoughts, and behaviors. They know how to bolster their own morale with realistic expectations of themselves, others, and even God. They know that God never does for priests what they can do for themselves. They are enabled by the grace of their calling to offer encouragement and hope to others. They model self-confidence and hope, sending a powerful message to other people from which they in turn may derive self-confidence and hope. They experience high levels of trust, acceptance and even intimacy throughout their ministries.

Such grace-filled roots produce Christ-like fruits, namely, a growing sense of wholeness and holiness. The priest can prevent his own boredom and burnout, renewing, revitalizing, enriching, and transforming himself in Christ through ministry.

PRIEST AS BEARER OF THE MYSTERY

Robert E. Barron

This is an extremely difficult time for priests. With the revelations of clergy sexual misconduct with children and adolescents, and with the resignations of prominent bishops after scandalous violations of the celibacy vow, some priests have gone beyond the point of shock and surprise to a state of numbness. Many wonder whether permanent damage has been done to the priesthood, whether we will ever recover the trust and confidence that have been lost. Some speculate that vocations will plummet or that this is the beginning of the end of the priesthood as we know it. My own view is that such problems are symptomatic of a much more fundamental loss of confidence in the priesthood, a loss that can and must be regained.

Too many priests feel at sea without focus and orientation, without spiritual moorings, unable to articulate for themselves who they are and why they remain faithful to their commitments. In the postconciliar period, myriad new ministers have appeared on the church scene, and there has been much enthusiastic definition and clarification of their roles; the laity have been enabled and commissioned—brought to much greater involvement. All of this change has been healthy and revitalizing for the church. But many priests feel that in the process, their role has been diminished and their unique contribution undervalued. The feeling has led, at least in part, to the general malaise so much in evidence today.

I write from the profound conviction that the crisis of confidence should lead not to speculations about the collapse of the priesthood but to a renewed commitment to the priesthood and to a deeper understanding of its nature, purpose, and spirituality. This is not the time for hand-wringing but for renewed thinking, dreaming, and imagining. We must return to the sources—to the heart and soul of priesthood—if we are to recover the meaning and power of the priesthood in the life of the church.

The Priest as Bearer of Mystery

Let me propose a model, or better, an image which I believe captures something of the unique and indispensable quality of the priesthood. The priest of Jesus Christ is, first and foremost, a mystagogue, one who bears the Mystery and initiates others into it. At the heart of the Christian faith is a confrontation with the all-grounding and all-encompassing mystery of Being itself, which is God. The believer is grasped, shaken, overwhelmed by that powerful force, which in Jesus Christ is revealed as wild, passionate, unconditional love. Without a sense of that ever fascinating and uncontrollable power, the church becomes, at best, a social welfare organization or a self-help society.

The priest is the one who bears that strange power and who leads the people of God into an ever more intimate contact with it. In carrying out this task, one is most authentically a priest, that is, the one who performs the sacrifice linking heaven and earth, mediating between the Mystery and those who have been grasped by it. Christ is the High Priest because, in his own person, he is the reconciliation of creation and Creator, the mediation between Lover and beloved. In the depths of his being the mystagogue is conformed to Christ the priest, shaped according to the icon of Christ; the priest's whole existence is to become transparent to the Mystery.

The primary function of the bearer of Mystery is to hold up to the people of God the great images, stories, and pictures of salvation that lie at the heart of the Christian tradition. The mystagogue is the one who has been entrusted with the sacred symbols and given the responsibility of making them speak. He is the artist whose task is to make the liturgy a great dance expressive of God's grace, a stunning saga at the heart of which is God's embrace of every aspect of our fallen humanity. Through manipulation of color, line, and texture, the painter unveils some truth about nature or about the human condition and invites the viewer to enter into that truth. In a similar way, the mystagogical artist, in image, symbol, and story, presents the truth that is God's love in Christ and draws the worshipping community to share in it. In James Joyce's *A Portrait of the Artist as a Young Man,* the protagonist, Stephen Dedalaus, is grasped by a vision of the beautiful and feels compelled to abandon everything in order to become a creator and mediator of beauty. The mystagogue of God's beauty is grasped by the same power and has the same vocation.

This artistic or iconic role presupposes that the priest is deeply in touch with the genius of the Catholic imagination. The Catholic vision is based, philosophically, on the *analogia entis,* the analogy or continuity between the being of the world and the Being that is God. Theologically, the vision is rooted in the Incarnation, God's radical union with Jesus of Nazareth and his entry, by implication, into the whole of the cosmos. According to this view of things, God is present everywhere in the universe; hints and traces of divine love are "spread out on the earth" for those who have the eyes to see them. Bernanos's country priest was seized by the Catholic imagination when he announced, in the face of his enormous suffering and disappointment: "Everything is grace."

The priest, if he is to mediate the Mystery, must be gifted with the Catholic imagination and must be a lifelong apprentice of those throughout the centuries who have been in the grip of the Catholic sensibility. He must develop an eye that can see the Incarnate God in the dome of the Hagia Sophia, in the spires at the Chartres Cathedral, in the athletes and prophets on the Sistine Chapel ceiling, in the light that illumines Carravagio's figures, in Giotto's frescoes of Saint Francis, and in the stained glass of the Sainte Chapelle. The mystagogue must be an artist filled with the light and energy of the Incarnation, and his vision must be contagious. G.K. Chesterton said that, to see the world properly, one must stand on one's head. Seeing everything as hanging upside down, one sees it as it is, literally dependent on the Creator God. The mystagogue is the one who dedicates his life to standing upside down in order to share that peculiar vision with the church.

PRIEST AS TEACHER & PREACHER

The one who bears the Mystery must be both teacher and preacher. In Christ, God has spoken the definitive word of love. Conformed personally and existentially to that word, the priest speaks of and from the experience of being grasped by God. Paul Tillich says that one cannot help but speak about what concerns one ultimately. The priest is the seer and poet who cannot help but speak the ultimate concern which is God's unreasonable and excessive love. Like Isaiah, his lips have been seared by the fire of God's mind, and like Ezekiel he has tasted the word, taken it into his flesh and bones, and has found it at once sweet and overwhelming. Study after study has shown that the people in the pews want, above all, good preaching from their priests. It seems to me that this altogether reasonable demand reflects a hunger and thirst for mystagogy, a desire to be told of the Mystery and drawn into it.

The preacher of the word must be conformed to the Word, which is Jesus Christ, and must therefore be a lifelong student not only of the Scripture but also of the great literary expressions of Catholic sensibility. He must be able to appreciate the Incarnational spirituality in the autobiographies of Augustine, Merton, and Teresa of Avila; he must feel with the otherworld journey of Dante and with the bawdy worldliness of the Canterbury Tales; he must be able to share the anguish in the verse of Gerard Manley Hopkins and T. S. Eliot; he must enter into the vision of Peguy and Claudel and climb the mountains that are Dostoevski and Joyce.

THE PRIEST SET APART

If the priest is to be a mediator between heaven and earth, if he is to speak symbolically of the all-embracing and ever elusive mystery of Being itself, he must be in habitual contact with the Mystery, he must stand stubbornly in the presence of God. He must take with utmost seriousness the command of Saint Paul to pray continually, to orient the whole of his being to the love of God. In short, the priest must be a mystic, a contemplative, a person of prayer. This is hardly the unique vocation of a monk; it is the parish priest, the privileged mystagogue, who must be, in every fiber of his being, formed by prayer.

Simply put, the priest must be an authentically religious leader for his people; he must be, in the richest sense possible, spiritual director, mystical guide, shaman. I think that one of the greatest postconciliar mistakes was to turn the priest into psychologist, sociologist, social worker, counselor, and anything but a uniquely religious leader. The authentic task of the mystagogue, as I've outlined it, is incomparably rich and constantly challenging. It is the career of the prophet, poet, and visionary. Why would we want to abandon such a role for that of psychologist or social worker?

Is such a view of the priesthood elitist, too intellectual, or rather monkish? Is all this literary and artistic refinement fine for the seminary or university professor but unrealistic for the parish priest? Not in my view. For it is precisely the parish priest who has most contact with, and influence upon, the people of God. Therefore, it is precisely the parish priest who should be best equipped to know, mediate, and express the Mystery. Sophistication of mind, heart, and sensibility is no luxury for the parish priest. Rather, it belongs to the very essence of who he is and what he does.

In the preconciliar period, the official theology of the church spoke of an "ontological change" that occurs at ordination: the priest does not simply receive the commission to perform specific tasks, he becomes someone different. This language, understood as elitist and exclusionary, has unfortunately fallen into desuetude. Rather than misinterpreting the terminology of ontological change as clericalism, one should embrace the truth enshrined in the formulation. For the mystagogue is not primarily a functionary, not someone entrusted with tasks to perform. He is priest, someone who in his very being is the mediator between heaven and earth. Called and formed by God for the service of the community, the mystagogue is separate, unique, set apart, in the language of Scripture, holy. Priesthood affects one in one's very being, else it is a sham. Understood as a job or a ministry, priesthood becomes a shadow of itself and loses its fascination and appeal.

Andrew Greeley is correct in saying that priests are irresistibly fascinating and that the fascination flows from the uniqueness and peculiarity of their being. Those who want to demythologize the language of ontological change and conceive of the priest as only one minister among many are flying in the face of something which lies in the blood and bones of the race, something in the deepest religious instincts of human beings. Across cultures and throughout history, people have always designated certain of their number as "holy ones," as mediators of the Mystery. And it has always been precisely that separateness, that uniqueness of existence, which has enabled the "holy one" to be transparent to God or to the gods.

One of the shortest routes to the desacralization of the Catholic community is the "functionalization" of the priesthood. The great Protestant preacher and hymn writer John Wesley once described his preaching style: "I set myself on fire and people come out and watch me burn." That could also serve as a description of the ontological nature of the priesthood. The priest is not, primarily, someone who works, preaches, ministers, counsels; rather he is someone who—at the core of his being—has been set on fire by God, and who invites others to catch the flame.

CELIBACY AS AN ACT OF LOVE

Only against such a vision of priesthood can the celibacy of the priest be properly grasped and appreciated. When one tries to justify celibacy on functional grounds, the arguments sound tinny and unconvincing. For example, it is suggested that celibacy frees one for a greater range of ministry. This might be true in some cases, but it could be argued just as persuasively that the support of spouse, children, and home life enables the married minister to serve more effectively than any celibate. Some have claimed that the celibate can love more universally and disinterestedly than the married clergy. And while it might be true for some, one could argue that the especially rich love of family that characterizes the married minister intensifies and augments love for the congregation and for others. By comparison, the pastoral affection of the celibate for his people could seem superficial.

The issue of celibacy is not convincing when based on practical or even pastoral considerations. It is only when celibacy is seen as altogether impractical and absurd that we can begin adequately to understand it.

Paul Tillich offers a fascinating reading of the scriptural account of the woman who breaks open the jar of perfume to anoint the feet of Jesus, in the face of the reasonable objections of the disciples. Tillich says that the woman represents the unreasonable or excessive element that must be part of the response to one's ultimate concern. Tillich's view makes ridiculous Kant's suggestion that religion could be understood "within the limits of reason alone." When one has been seized by the infinite and unconditional love of God, one responds in an excess of love, in an unreasonable, disproportionate, even scandalous self-offering. According to reasonable and sober reflection like that of the disciples, the woman's excessive act can seem inappropriate or bizarre, but it is her excessive love that is praised and welcomed by Christ.

Celibacy is unreasonable, unnatural, and excessive, which is why it has been chosen, across cultures and throughout history, as one of the ways in which lovers of God have traditionally expressed their love. To try to understand this self-gift or explain it is to miss the point. Its very strangeness and incomprehensibility is the point. Not surprisingly, mystagogues, those who have been chosen by the Mystery to speak of the Mystery, see the appropriateness of this excessive stance and lifestyle. Called to stand on the horizon between heaven and earth, set afire by the presence of God, the mystagogue rather naturally chooses the unnatural option of celibacy. People in love do strange things.

This very strangeness is what gives celibacy its witness value. In the Incarnation, the ultimacy of the world was thrown radically into question. The presence of God in Christ shook and uprooted the "self-complacent finitude" of sinners, turning us toward that power which is ever greater than we can think, feel, or imagine. The Christ reveals that the deepest love a human being can experience is the love for the infinite Being, who grounds the universe and transcends time. Our destiny is not limited to the enjoyment of goods or pleasures in this life; rather, the most basic and powerful orientation of our spirits is toward the undreamed of richness of God's life.

The celibate priest is someone who, in the strangeness of his choice of lifestyle, reminds the people of God of their profoundest destiny, so easily lost sight of in our secularistic and materialistic culture. The celibate priest is that poet and prophet who, in his being, speaks of the uncanniness of the Reality which has seized us, who reminds us that perhaps "something else might be the case."

This brief reflection offers no solution, per se, to the crisis of confidence in the priesthood. What I offer here is an image of the priest as mystagogue, an image which comes close to the heart of what the priesthood, at its best, has always been. Were he conformed to

Christ and confirmed in his role as mystagogue, it would be difficult for the priest to be bored in his work and way of life. The authentic bearer of the Mystery, the one living on the frontier between God and creation, the "hero" who journeys from earth to heaven and from heaven to earth, is not likely to find his life tedious or void of meaning.

I believe passionately in the centrality and indispensability of the mystagogue in the community gathered around Jesus Christ. What could kill us as a church is losing the sense of Mystery. What could contribute mightily to that loss is the weakening and dissipation of the priesthood. The time has come not for dismantling the priesthood but for building it up.

Priest as Doctor of the Soul

Robert E. Barron

As many commentators have pointed out, there is a crisis of confidence and identity among priests today. Many new ministries and roles of service have emerged in the church, and laypeople are assuming, legitimately, many of the tasks formerly performed exclusively by the clergy. It has led some priests to wonder what their unique contribution might be, what they, distinctively, can offer to the people of God. In "Priest as Bearer of the Mystery," I presented the vision of priest as mystagogue, as the one who guides people into the grounding and sustaining mystery which is God. The mystagogue, I argued, is the artist and poet who fires hearts with the power of the Catholic imagination, the shaman who lures people into a confrontation with the Mystery that suffuses and transcends all our experience. The priest is not so much psychologist or social worker as he is spiritual leader, pastor of the soul, the one who leads people to a discovery of that deepest self which is in living contact with God.

DOCTOR OF THE SOUL

That description of the priest's "task" is, I think, correct but incomplete. Before a person can be conducted into the Mystery that is God, he or she must be healed of whatever spiritual ill, whatever block, prevents the journey of self-surrender. Closely related to the role of mystagogue, then, is "doctor of the soul."

The Gospels are filled with accounts of Jesus' healing encounters with those whose spiritual energies are unable to flow. Much of his ministry consisted in teaching people how to see (the kingdom of God), how to hear (the voice of the Spirit), how to walk (thereby overcoming the paralysis of the heart), how to be free of themselves so as to discover God. Jesus was referred to in the early church as the savior (*soter* in Greek and *salvator* in Latin), terms that speak of the one who brings healing (our word *salve* is closely related to the Latin *salvus,* meaning health). Christ is the "bringer of the salve," the carrier of the healing balm. In imitation of Christ, the priest is the doctor of the soul, the healer of broken hearts and minds.

The "soul" is that stillpoint at the heart of every person, that deepest center, that point of encounter with the transcendent yet incarnate mystery of God. It is that level on which we are grasped by what Paul Tillich calls "ultimate concern." It corresponds to what the church Fathers call the *imago Dei,* the image of God. It is the ground and source of all psychological and physical energy; it is the matrix and organizing power of the human person. When the soul is healthy, it is in a living relationship with God; it is firmly rooted in the soil of meaning and is the deepest center of the person. But when the soul is sick, the link to the energy and being of God is severed or at least rendered tenuous. When the soul is sick, the entire person becomes ill because all flows from and depends on the dynamic encounter with the source of being and life who is God. It is this intimate link between the soul and the psyche that C.G. Jung implicitly acknowledged when he remarked that, at bottom, all psychological problems are religious problems.

But what sort of "medicine" is prescribed by the priest as soul doctor? How does he unleash blocked spiritual energies and heal the wounds of the soul? The answer, it seems to me, is the energy, the power, the spirit, the new being, that appeared in and through Jesus Christ. We heal the soul by bringing to bear the *salvator,* the healer, the one who in his person reconciled God and us, who opened soul to the divine power. Where is this new being available? It is apparent in the Scriptures, liturgy, sacraments, Christian architecture, painting and literature—and, in perhaps most rarefied form, in Christian doctrines.

These bearers of the new being—these prolongations of the energy of Christ—are the "medicines" employed by the priest, the healing balms by which soul sickness is cured. They are "symbols of

transformation" whose primary purpose is to change the lives of
Christians by drawing them into the *imitatio Christi*. In various ways
the priest holds up the icon of Jesus Christ in the hope that all who see
it will be transfigured into its likeness.

Consider a concrete example drawn from the spiritual tradition.
When one prays before an icon of Jesus, one enters into a subtle
process of "consciousness transformation." The one who contemplates
the icon is not simply diverted by a pious representation, but assumes
the stance, adopts the vision, mimics the attitude, thinks the thoughts
and senses the emotions of the depicted figure. As a result, the mind
and heart are reworked in a sort of alchemical process; the entire person is reconfigured through a spiritual osmosis. In the presence of the
icon of the Lord, the pray-er experiences literal *metanoia* (going beyond
the mind), finding a whole new perspective.

The doctor of the soul also indicates the icon of the New Being
in Jesus Christ in order to effect such a psychospiritual metamorphosis.
To shift the image somewhat, the priest as soul doctor rubs in the salve
of the Incarnation to heal the wounds of the soul.

Consider one of the "medicines" mentioned above: the dogmas
and theological teachings of the tradition. On the face of it, these
abstract and conceptual formulas seem unlikely candidates as mediators
of soul transformation. I've become more and more convinced, however, that theology as practiced by the great masters of our tradition is
anything but a recondite, abstract discipline or mind-game. Instead,
dogmas and theological formulations are meant to lure the believer
onto healthy spiritual ground, to orient him or her to the God who is
really God, not an idol. Precisely because dogmatic statements are so
spiritually charged, they have been at the heart of some of the greatest
struggles in the history of the church.

THE "MEDICINE" OF THE INCARNATION

The doctrine at the heart of the Christian experience that possesses the
greatest transformative power is the Incarnation. What does it mean for
someone to be grasped by this dogma, to be shaken and turned around
by it? To live in the energy of the Incarnation is to know real union
with God, in the depth of one's humanity. Jesus Christ, the Incarnate
Word, demonstrates to the world that the human being is made for

God and finds rest only in God. Jesus reveals that God wants nothing more than to come to life in us, to become incarnate in our words and actions, in our thoughts, fears and insecurities. The Incarnation means that nothing of our humanity is alien to God or untouched by divine power: birth, coming of age, rejection, friendship, betrayal, anxiety, bliss, the frightful darkness of death, triumph—all of it becomes, in principle, a route of access to the transcendent reality. Because of the coming together of the divine and human in Jesus, we have the courage to explore a new and deeper identity, one rooted, not in the petty desires and fears of the ego but in the eternal power and existence of God.

The assumption is that the language of the Incarnation is not meant simply to describe a strange and distant event, to speak a truth concerning Jesus alone. As the great medieval mystic, Meister Eckhart, has written, if the Word does not come to birth in us today, it is no use reading about the incarnation of that Word in a person long ago. If, in short, we ourselves do not participate in who Jesus was, we miss the spiritual power he unleashed. Jesus does not want worshipers but followers, or better, participants: "I am the vine and you are the branches"; "live on in me"; "my body is real food and my blood real drink"; "the one who feeds on my flesh and drinks my blood remains in me and I in him." These beautifully organic images that Saint John presents are meant to communicate the life-changing power of the Incarnation: the Logos became flesh, our flesh, so that we might allow the divine energy to be born in us.

It is summed up in the oft-repeated patristic adage that God became human that humans might become God. Many great theologians and spiritual masters speak unselfconsciously of "divinization," a sharing in the symbiosis that is the Incarnation, as the proper goal of human life.

Having taken the doctrine of the Incarnation off its dusty academic shelf, we can see how it functions as a healing balm at the disposal of the doctor of the soul. The Incarnation is the "salve" applied to one who has lost his center, his existential bearings, his identity. At such times we sometimes cling to ourselves out of fear, rooting our lives in the desires and impulses of the ego rather than in the infinite reality of God. We refuse to surrender to the power of the divine, convinced that we will find meaning and focus in reliance upon our own egos. In many ways, this sinful attitude is characteristic of our time and manifests itself in the widespread feelings of rootlessness, meaningless-ness, anxiety, and despair.

What the doctor of the soul can bring to such sickness is some-thing no psychologist or physician can bring: what the priest can offer is the good news and energy of the Incarnation. He can hold out to the sufferer the possibility of participating in the God who wants nothing more than to embrace the human condition. He can invite the person in anxiety or despair to root her life, not in herself, but in eternity, in the transcendent ground of meaning which is the creator God; he can offer her the body and blood, the life of Jesus Christ. Again, this has not primarily to do with accepting doctrines intellectually; rather, it involves sharing in the power of transformation.

THE HEALING POWER OF THE SIMPLE GOD

All Christian doctrines flow from the central teaching of the Incarnation, including and especially the doctrine of God. Many of the most significant Christian theologians insist on dismantling the mythology of God as the "supreme being." Augustine, Origen, pseudo-Dionysius, Thomas Aquinas, Anselm, and, in modern times, Paul Tillich and Karl Rahner all hold that God is not "a being," not even the highest being, but rather Being itself, the infinite, all-grounding, all-enveloping power of existence. God can in no way be quantified or qualified or described in the categories that define the things of the world. Thomas Aquinas sums up his teaching by saying that God is "altogether simple." He means that God is not a type of being, not an instance of being, not a thing in any sort of category, not one being among others, but rather that which simply is.

Why have Christian theologians from the earliest centuries spo-ken this way of God? The answer is found in the shock and surprise of the Incarnation. The first Christians experienced in Jesus that the divine and the human had come unspeakably close, and that Christ's humanity was not suppressed but preserved and enhanced through his union with God. This means that God cannot be a rival or competitor to human beings, not something standing over and against us, but rather something totally other, a power beyond and outside the "nor-mal" relations of finitude. The God who becomes incarnate in Jesus Christ cannot be one more "thing in the world," capable of being avoided or, worse, manipulated and controlled. No, the God of the Incarnation is that absolute, infinite, transcendent/immanent power of Being itself that continually lures us into greater life and more plentiful existence. In no sense a "competitor," the simple God is the one who, in her otherness, opens up the human heart.

Christian theologians have for so long stressed the strangeness of God precisely because they want to escape the danger of idolatry. Idolatry is at the heart of the sinner's strategy to reduce God to the level of a being, even the "supreme being," since such a reality cannot be of decisive and transformative significance. An idol can be relegated to the distant past or placed at an infinite remove from us—"up there" or "out there" somewhere. Such a God is what the Old Testament calls an idol, a false god, a projection of the sinful human desire to be the absolute. The simple God, the divine power that appears in Jesus Christ, is that which cannot be controlled, cannot be set aside, cannot be ignored, cannot be turned into an idol. "Thou mastering me God," is Gerard Manley Hopkins's magnificent address to the reality who will not be turned into a false god.

Once again, such a clarification is not simply a more "correct" description of the nature of God. On the contrary, it is a matter of spiritual life or death. The paradigmatic sin of the Old Testament is idolatry, turning something which is not God into God, or better, reducing the absolute to the level of the contingent and finite. The Old Testament authors—and even more intensely, the Christian theological authors—were so concerned with this problem precisely because idolatry amounts to a shrinking of the soul. When the final reality of one's life is transformed into a "thing," the soul's access to the infinite has been denied, the proper destiny of the soul to transcend itself indefinitely has been suppressed. In one form or another, all spiritual problems are forms of this basic drying-up of the soul, modes of this "self-complacent finitude." Whether the absolute has assumed the form of sex, relationship, job, wealth, status, religion, the esteem of others, the spiritual sickness is the same: idolatry, a drying up of the soul's energies.

What does the priest as doctor of the soul bring to this sickness, which is perhaps manifesting itself as depression, loss of focus, anxiety, or compulsive behavior? He brings the healing balm of God's simplicity. In light of the power that flows from the Incarnation, he holds up to the sufferer the one reality that truly is absolute, the one power that truly can satisfy the longings of the heart, the God who is not a "thing" at all, but rather the ground and goal of Being itself. The soul doctor applies the salve of God's ungraspable, inescapable reality in order to quell the clinging tendencies of the ego and thereby to re-orient the spiritual energies of the sufferer. One could say that the essence of sin is an absolutizing of the ego; and one could consequently argue that the essence of soul-healing is a questioning of that inflated ego in light of the simple God.

THE SALVE OF CREATION

A central Christian teaching that has flowed from the doctrine of the simple God is that of creation, or more precisely, creation *ex nihilo,* from nothing. According to this dogma, God continually creates and grounds the world, pouring being into it as a free gift. The things of the world do not stand over and against God as if they were fundamentally independent of him; rather, every moment they stand as sheer receptivity, literally as "nothing," accepting the grace that is their existence. In both classical and modern Christian theologies of creation, the creator God does not stand simply "at the beginning of time," as if he brought the world into being and then simply left it to its own devices. On the contrary, the God who is Being creates and renews the world unceasingly, pouring it out of himself in a great act of super-abundant love.

What does this doctrine mean spiritually? How does it embody in some way the good news of Jesus Christ? The philosophical dogma of creation *ex nihilo* shows the believer how to root herself in the springs of life and meaning. To affirm that one is a creature is to feel, almost literally in one's bones, that one's entire being is a gift from a transcendent source. This doctrine teaches that at the center of who I am is a relationship of pure openness to the God who is giving himself in pure love. If I am a creature, then I am not a "thing" that confronts God; rather, I am a relation of joyful receptivity to the inrushing passion of the divine source. Everything that I am flows from this relation and is centered upon it.

Thomas Merton writes that the heart of contemplative prayer is the discovery of that point at the root and core of my being where I am, here and now, being created by God. To pray is to realize profoundly that I am at every moment a creature, a child of God. The doctrine of creation is meant to be an icon of spiritual identity, a living reminder that I am called to find myself in an act of obedient surrender to the sustaining and self-offering ground of being. In short, creation is "soul" language, a description of what it means for my center to be linked in a living union with the center of all existence.

What happens when someone loses touch with his own creatureliness? On the one hand, he might sink into despair since he has lost contact with the eternal wellspring of his being and identity. He might sense that his life has been drained of meaning, that he is cut off, adrift in a hostile world. Or he might experience ego inflation as he tries to turn his achievements and accomplishments into the ground of his life. This latter stance can lead to what Paul Tillich calls the concupiscent attitude. Caught in concupiscence, a person wants to "shove the whole world into his mouth," attempting to fill up the void within with money, fame, power, sex, etc. The whole addictive style can be an outgrowth or symptom of the fundamentally spiritual problem.

Faced with such sicknesses of the soul, the priest as healer can hold up the icon of creation *ex nihilo.* Under the influence of this "salve," one comes to see that he is essentially nothing, that his all-powerful ego is a phantom or illusion, a creation of his desire. When he realizes that he is a creature, in every aspect of his being a gift from God, he can let go, relax his grip, stem his concupiscence. As a creature, he is centered and rooted in that power of being that is beyond space and time, beyond the vagaries and dangers of the world. Nothing but a relation to the creator God, he can say with Paul, "for I am certain that neither death nor life, neither angels nor principalities, neither height nor depth, nor any other creature could ever separate me from the love of God." Such assurance of the soul is something that no psychologist or physician could bring. It is the healing balm offered by the doctor of the spirit.

CONCLUSION

I have tried to show how the priest can recover and reclaim an ancient identity by accepting the responsibility of soul doctoring. I have also indicated what sort of tools and medicines he might use in the process:

Incarnation, the divine simplicity, and creation from nothing. These are not merely abstractions for the mind, but in their original and most important form are, like all the other great doctrines, symbols of transformation, icons that illumine the spirit. Like the other articles of the creed, they are bearers of the healing power that flows from Jesus Christ.

It has struck me that often Christian leaders and spiritual directors tragically fail to realize the treasure that is theirs, the wealth of wisdom stored on dusty shelves and buried in arid doctrinal formulas. The priest should drink deeply from the wells of that tradition and rediscover its enormous potential for opening up the hearts and spirits of those he serves. In soul doctoring, he might also recover a richer sense of himself and his identity as a priest.

ONGOING PROFESSIONAL DEVELOPMENT
A Ministerial Imperative

Matthias Neuman

It has become almost commonplace to say that the Catholic church in the United States has been and is going through a time of transition and turbulence. Many reasons have been adduced to explain the upheavals, confusions, and hostilities of the past two decades: the effects of the Second Vatican Council, the influence of secularization, and the erosion of religious commitment in general. It will probably take the distance of decades or even generations to assess all the reasons for the changes of our era. But whatever the causes, the effects of the last quarter century on American Catholicism have been vividly described by the Reverend Andrew Greeley as a "Rembrandt landscape after a storm." However one expresses it, we do live in a diverse, fragmented, often polarized church. Differences of approach between reactionaries and radicals, conservatives and liberals, color every aspect of church life. Where all this is moving, what the future holds, and how these various positions will resolve their differences remains a puzzle. Nonetheless, this is the cultural environment of American Catholicism within which most parish ministers work. It is an environment fraught with doubts, contrasting opinions, and conflicts both within and without the church.

To labor in this context places a special stress upon pastoral ministers: they must often do their work in the absence of an initial trust and welcome not only from the people they serve but also from other ministers with whom they must work. For example, one of the first dynamics upon meeting a new minister of any variety is discerning "where he or she stands." It can become an ecclesiastical poker game: "I won't show my hand until you show yours." Many priests, DREs, and pastoral associates will confirm that mutual suspicion often describes the initial attitude of encounter among parish ministers. The games played can be quite humorous at times: the strained effort of casual questioning at the dinner table to find where another priest stands on touchy issues, or sisters deliberately placing a sexist text before a retreat master to force him to show his hand.

These stories and episodes can be funny, but beneath them lie an attitude of suspicion and testing and a withholding of support until the new minister proves himself or herself to be credible. This spells massive problems for the development of good ministry. Such an attitude will not permit any real collaboration, for the new individual receives neither the benefit of the doubt nor the affirmation that comes with it. Suspicion hinders smooth transition and new bondings and can sour a young minister just beginning a career.

The newly arrived minister is challenged to prove a love for and commitment to the faith and life of the people to be served. Sometimes the new or inexperienced minister must demonstrate his or her credibility to colleagues and congregations before it is reciprocated.

John F. Fletcher, in *Religious Authenticity in the Clergy* (The Alban Institute, 1975), describes three stages in what he calls a process of religious authentication. There is first an examining or testing of the personal strengths of the minister to see if there is enough personal depth to justify a further step or relationship. The second stage probes the minister's professional authenticity: does the minister have the appropriate skills to benefit the lives of the people? With the third stage comes acceptance, as the minister becomes part of the community and its individual religious lives. Only in this last stage will the people be willing to trust his or her leadership. Pastoral ministers laboring in today's Catholic cultural context should expect to pass through this gauntlet of testing several times as they move from position to position. Spiritual preparation will be needed to help make transitions well.

A second aspect of the United States context which influences pastoral ministry is that Catholics have by and large entered fully into the mainstream of our nation's larger cultural life. Many social and historical studies have noted the passing of immigrant Catholicism and its isolationist mentality. This assimilating process, begun after World War

II, wrought major changes in the makeup of U.S. Catholicism. Following a quantum leap in educational opportunities, U.S. Catholics became in the span of one generation the most educated laity in the history of the church. This sudden jump generated problems. For while secular education led to college and postgraduate degrees, religious education often remained at the level of primary or secondary schooling. The result is a large group of Catholics who, stimulated by university studies, are able to ask sharp and sophisticated questions, but who often lack the solid intellectual faith foundation from which to draw material for answers. A finely tuned motor sputters on inferior gas.

Consider a sampling of questions I encountered in the space of three months. These are the concerns of average parishioners carrying on their lives of faith in several small Midwestern towns: "What is the relation of Islam to Christianity, especially in its evaluation of Jesus?" (asked by a farmer after viewing a television news program on Iran and Islam). "What is the sacramentality of the renewal of baptismal vows during the Easter Vigil?" (asked by an office worker during an adult education class). "What relation does the ancient covenant of God with the Jewish people have to the 'new' covenant that Christianity speaks of?" (asked by a hotel manager after a discussion with a Jewish guest).

Needless to say, these are not easy questions even for someone with years of theological education. Conscientious answers will require research, reflection, and discussion with scholars.

ONE BELIEF SYSTEM AMONG MANY

But the United States context goes even further. As many Catholics entered the mainstream of American life through higher education, they found their faith confronted by the worldviews of other religious faiths as well as by the powerful arguments of modern secular thought. Values learned and inculcated in the safe havens of family and local parish were thrown against the sharp rocks of competing value systems in a public forum. In the local, rural region where I live, this same challenge remains present in the lives of many young people attending the state universities for the first time. There students discover people with views that contradict and deny much of what they were taught to believe and hold sacred. Many American Catholic families suffered and still live with the remains of shipwrecked beliefs.

Cultural challenge as a whole has implications for the style and content of contemporary pastoral ministry. As educated laity search more and more for intelligibility in their faith, for understandings based in history and scholarship and presented in understandable contemporary language, they deserve sound theology to help them deal with problems of life and faith. Presenting sound theology is an essential part of modern ministerial work. The thirst for a contemporary and intellectually credible formulation of Catholic faith presents a pressing need, which affects all pastoral ministry. Similarly many Catholics seek the confidence and skills to hold and sharpen their own faith while dialoguing with those with other religious beliefs in our modern pluralistic society. Television, conferences, and bookstores bring people in touch with numerous varieties of religious belief. Many Catholic adults deeply appreciate their own faith, but also wish to extend tolerance toward others. They will not automatically dismiss a view, whether New Age or spiritualism, for they know their children, family members, or friends may consider it seriously. In sum, a large portion of today's Catholics seek a truly Catholic Christian identity, one not only rooted solidly in its own history and beliefs, but able to sustain a living dialogue with other faiths.

CATHOLICISM ON SOLID GROUND

Therefore, pastoral ministers have a particular obligation to study seriously the historical meanings and contemporary expressions of faith. The basic conviction that every parish pastoral minister is an intellectual witness to the Catholic tradition needs to be strongly affirmed. Our current generation of ministers-in-training will have to hit the books hard to avoid the painful results of ignoring the theological underpinnings of the church's faith. Those entering any program of ministry formation, from seminary to diocesan lay institute, must be challenged to delve deeply into hard, critical approaches to theological subjects. This would include, at least, some understanding of historical and literary investigation in Scripture, a critical approach to church history, a social science perspective on ecclesiology, and an awareness of Catholic liturgical traditions as seen through historical and symbolic methodology.

All pastoral ministers should commit themselves to regular self-examination about the hard thinking and investigation they undertake on the problems of living the faith as a Catholic today. They should be able to offer a response to their congregations that is historically and theologically grounded and intellectually reasonable.

CATHOLICS IN A MEDIA CULTURE

American Catholics live within an overpowering media culture which tries to sell, propagandize, and manipulate its audience into becoming docile subjects waiting to be entertained. Compelling visions of modern advertising have created a pervasive "entertainment expectation." Every day newscasters, actors, athletes, celebrities, and writers project their personalities onto the awareness of modern Americans, leading to the demand for a faith not only formulated in contemporary language but also expressed with a flair and conviction requisite to a media culture. American consciousness is patterned and dominated by the visual media; it responds first to "how" material is expressed (emotionally, enthusiastically, colorfully), long before giving thought to its truth. A faith presented without power and style will often be dismissed without a deeper look.

Faith expressed in a media society must be delivered not only with heartfelt conviction, but also with accomplished skills of public proclamation that engage heart, mind, and imagination. One who proclaims the gospel is compared (albeit subconsciously) to Tom Brokaw, Connie Chung, and a host of other media personalities. The question for proclaimers is: Do you really have your heart and soul in it? People don't see intentions; rather they feel and absorb the power and skill put into a message through language, imagery, and rhetorical skills. Developing and improving those skills is a regular challenge to the pastoral minister laboring within today's media culture.

Psychology dominates the awareness of Americans: the need— even prestige—of having a psychiatrist or a psychologist, or having read a list of self-help books that offer psychological answers to every human problem. Pastoral ministry generally includes some attempt at "public help," a kind of poor person's psychiatric or social agency. What's more, people demand from the pastoral minister a deep empathy and identification with their own problems. It will not do to deal with people in a detached, purely professional way; our psychological world demands a respectful, attentive listening. Whether in counseling, confession, spiritual direction, or in-depth conversation, the modern minister discovers a panorama of relationships that all cry out for sensitive listening, acceptance, and appreciation. To be a sympathetically attuned minister puts a great drain on one's psychic powers.

The increasing literature on burnout in all the helping professions, religious and secular, attests to the highly psychologized and volatile world the contemporary pastoral minister enters. It is a different age from that of the doctrinaire teacher and sacramental presider of the immigrant church; today's psychological world spends more time righting the interior wrongs of failed love, betrayal, hostility, and apathy. This psychic overload saps the minister's own spiritual balance and health. It is an issue that must receive more attention.

CONTINUING EDUCATION FOR PASTORAL MINISTERS

To work within these challenging demands will require a radically new vision of pastoral education and formation for all parish ministers. An adequate formation program can no longer remain only foundational (that is, providing merely the basic professional requirements), but must become continual, in-depth, and ongoing. The style of ministry preparation dating from immigrant Catholicism will not work. Unfortunately this remains the predominant style in many formation programs for priests, permanent deacons, and various lay ministries: the presentation of required basics with little follow-up offered or sought. It is a blueprint for failure.

In the immigrant Catholicism of the late-nineteenth and early-twentieth centuries, church leaders were faced with an exploding population, a lack of priests and local leaders, a frequently hostile society, and a great variety of ethnic groups who felt cut off from their roots and were looking for a new identity in a new land. To meet this situation the American bishops outlined a basic religious stance for the immigrant Catholic church. The stance had a distinctly isolationist flavor but perhaps it was the only one possible. Pastors built a fence around Catholic parish life and guarded the people against errors and the temptations of false religions and atheists. The pastor's responsibility (he was usually the only parish minister recognized in those days) was to keep the parish as an enclosed family and to get the people to do as many educational, civic, recreational, and religious activities as possible within its safe confines. Practically everything took place within the parish.

Religious teaching meant conveying basic truths (catechism) and emphasizing them without question or doubt. The priest was key; he was the single dominating teacher, leader, and authority in the parish. At the time this stance did work. A network of vibrant Catholic parishes was created around the country, which nourished the faith of millions and gave them protection against dangers that might weaken or destroy their faith.

But along came the great transition forged by the Second World War and its related social changes. The world forced the church to adapt and to seek new ways of living, nourishing, and preserving its faith. The result has been the conflicting situation described above, which cannot be dealt with satisfactorily by the once-and-for-all style of authority that served the immigrant parish. American culture has shifted and this has resulted in a new religious context for American Catholics, a context demanding a new language, new symbols, and a new pastoral stance. The need for ministers to take the time for regular significant spiritual and personal renewal is no longer a luxury but a necessity for survival. This renewal must touch the ministers' own personal relationship with God, their commitment to service of God's people, and their real love of ministry. The conviction needs to be instilled in all pastoral ministers—during their initial formation—that their basic education is only foundational and does not bring one to mastery of true ministry. Ministers must build within themselves a conviction of their own needs and develop the will and the sacrifices necessary to satisfy them.

In *Crossing the Boundary: Between Seminary and Parish* (The Alban Institute, 1980), Roy Oswald has some challenging thoughts for seminarians who are leaving their years of ministry training to engage in their first full-time parish assignments, but these words could well apply to any pastoral minister entering upon a first position:

> I have one clear recommendation to you. It has to do with your attitude about your education for ministry. If you truly believe that you haven't even begun to learn approximately 80 percent of what you need to know to be an effective pastor, you will begin parish ministry with a disposition that

will get you through the first five years of ministry. If, on the other hand, you think you've about got it all together, and simply need to touch it up here and there with some first-hand experience, you are on the way to a major depression one to three years down the pike. It's the difference between thinking you know all about something . . . and . . . bringing a genuine curiosity to a calling, determining to discover it more fully.

Oswald proposes some very specific suggestions for ministers, which convey the flavor of a ministerial style of formation that is regular, continual, and invigorating. Find a good mentor. Build adequate support systems for yourself. Regularly retool your skills in interpersonal and group dynamics. Get training in stress management. Find spiritual friends or a group to help you nourish your spiritual living. Check yourself often on collaborative skills. Deepen your appreciation of humor and use it. Regularly study your faith.

The context of American Catholic life is challenging and intimidating for the pastoral minister of today. Yet there are great riches to be gained and great labors to be achieved. The work and satisfaction of modern ministers—be they priest, religious, lay man or woman—will depend significantly on their interiorizing a style of formation that regularly checks, renews, challenges, and invigorates their own living of the faith and commitment to serve.

About the Contributors

Reverend James J. Bacik, a priest of the Diocese of Toledo, serves as campus minister and adjunct professor of humanities at the University of Toledo. This article is based on a talk given at the twenty-fifth anniversary convention of the National Federation of Priests' Councils.

Reverend Robert E. Barron, a priest of the Archdiocese of Chicago, is associate professor of systematic theology at Mundelein Seminary.

Reverend Michael J. Himes is an associate professor of theology at Boston College.

Reverend M. Edmund Hussey is the retired pastor of Saint Raphael Church, Springfield, Ohio.

Reverend Thomas J. Morgan is pastor of Christ the King Church, Haddonfield, New Jersey. He is also a New Jersey licensed psychologist, marriage and family therapist, and certified school psychologist.

Monsignor Philip J. Murnion, a priest of the Archdiocese of New York, is the director of the National Pastoral Life Center, New York City.

Reverend Matthias Neuman, O.S.B., is a professor of theology and member of Saint Meinrad Archabbey, St. Meinrad, Indiana.

Most Reverend George Niederauer is bishop of Salt Lake City, Utah. This article, published in the Summer 1991 issue of *CHURCH,* is based on a talk given to a meeting of the National Catholic Education Association and published in the organization's newsletter "Seminaries in Dialogue."

Reverend David N. Power, O.M.I., is professor of systematic theology and liturgy at the Catholic University of America, Washington, D.C.

Reverend Neal E. Quartier is a psychotherapist at the Personal Resource Center in Syracuse, New York.

Sheed & Ward

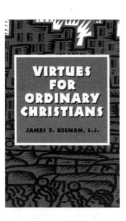

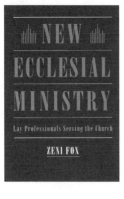